T0023508

First Food Responders

Praise for *First Food Responders*

ESG: Environmental, Social and Governance

In the parlance of sports, Alexia Parks and the company she runs would be characterized as a triple threat—namely, she feeds the hungry, assures that healthy food is provided, and creates jobs for those who lost their jobs at the height of the pandemic to carry forth this campaign. With both energy and courage, Alexia does not settle for the status quo and by so doing realizes her goal of doing the right thing, at the right time, in the right place.

—**Steven Lehat,** regulatory attorney and
strategic advisor to ESG companies

Finance and Economics

I have assisted many small business owners and reviewed many business plans. The First Food Responder model stands out because it creates jobs while tackling food insecurity without creating additional bureaucracy. It places no burden on government resources, is good for the economy, and is good for the environment. First Food Responders is a winner!

—**Howard O Bernstein,** Esq., CPA, past president
of the American Academy of Attorney-CPAs
and former associate regional advocate
for the US Small Business Administration

Energy and Air Pollution Reduction

I oversee programs that reduce the energy burden and carbon consumption of low-income residents of Riverside County. During the COVID-19 pandemic, I was tapped to begin sourcing and delivering meals to vulnerable unhoused residents. We ran this operation for four months before contracting with 23ZIP, Inc., home of the First Food Responders. It was then that I met Alexia Parks and was introduced to the First Food Responder model. As a professional dedicated to developing programs that meet people's needs and serve the greater community at the same time, I was immediately taken by the breadth of positive externalities of this model.

—**Wayne Harris,** energy program manager,
Community Action Partnership of Riverside County, California

Physical and Mental Health

I served as an advisor to this innovative food technology company in early 2021. I believe that the future of food is hyperlocal, fresh, healthy, and seasonal. I also believe that shared food experiences have the power to heal us and improve our physical, emotional, mental, and even spiritual well-being. I look forward to a future collaboration with First Food Responders!

—**Adam DeVito,** former director of new concept
development, Kraft Foods; managing partner,
Sterling-Rice Group; chairman, Monj Health

First Food Responders

People are Hungry.
Feed Them Now!
Here's How

Alexia Parks &
Joel Rauchwerger PhD
Former faculty at Baylor College of Medicine

NEW YORK

LONDON • NASHVILLE • MELBOURNE • VANCOUVER

First Food Responders

People are Hungry. Feed Them Now! Here's How

© 2023 Alexia Parks & Joel Rauchwerger PhD

All rights reserved. No portion of this book may be reproduced, stored in a retrieval system, or transmitted in any form or by any means—electronic, mechanical, photocopy, recording, scanning, or other—except for brief quotations in critical reviews or articles, without the prior written permission of the publisher.

Published in New York, New York, by Morgan James Publishing. Morgan James is a trademark of Morgan James, LLC. www.MorganJamesPublishing.com

Proudly distributed by Ingram Publisher Services.

Morgan James BOGO™

A **FREE** ebook edition is available for you or a friend with the purchase of this print book.

CLEARLY SIGN YOUR NAME ABOVE

Instructions to claim your free ebook edition:
1. Visit MorganJamesBOGO.com
2. Sign your name CLEARLY in the space above
3. Complete the form and submit a photo of this entire page
4. You or your friend can download the ebook to your preferred device

ISBN 9781631959943 paperback
ISBN 9781631959950 ebook
Library of Congress Control Number:
2022941327

Cover Design by:
Chris Treccani
www.3dogcreative.net

Interior Design by:
Christopher Kirk
www.GFSstudio.com

Morgan James PUBLISHING **Builds** with... **Habitat for Humanity** Peninsula and Greater Williamsburg

Morgan James is a proud partner of Habitat for Humanity Peninsula and Greater Williamsburg. Partners in building since 2006.

Get involved today! Visit MorganJamesPublishing.com/giving-back

Table of Contents

23ZIP Overview

2 3ZIP, Inc. is a public benefit corporation that is focused on empowering local communities, increasing access to fresh, healthy food, and teaching microenterprise home cooks how to help people eat better food. We're achieving this through both our First Food Responders™ (FFR) program, which is our first phase of training for individuals who want to learn more about healthy food choices, food safety, and our Zipper program, which is where they can graduate and be certified to run their own microenterprise business through our innovative technology platform.

Our goal is to address the top three problems in the US today, other than COVID.

The problems the 23ZIP government funded FFRs are fixing include:

- Feeding the food insecure. Providing fresh, healthy food to hungry people.
- Job security and a new career that gives FFRs enough money to pay their bills.
- Reducing income disparity and improving equity through a purpose-driven job.
- Dramatically lowing the carbon footprint in each community they serve.

To date, we have developed training courses and tutorials, gained traction in training both First Food Responders and Zippers, and prepared over 500,000 healthy meals through Project RoomKey. These meals have been delivered to 10 cities for two years throughout Riverside County, California, via Riverside County's Community Action Partnership) and Continuum of Care.

As a disruptive food-based business innovation and a technology platform, we link a diverse network of licensed certified home chefs who help create change through food in seven key areas.

- Create home-based jobs that offer a sustainable income.
- Improve community resilience and food security.
- Improve community health and nutrition.

- Reduce refined carbohydrates in a meal.
- Reduce animal-based protein to three ounces.
- Reduce food waste and water pollution.
- Reduce the carbon footprint and climate impact of transportation by making local, direct, seasonal food choices and preparing fresh, healthy homemade meals for pickup or delivery in their neighborhood or zip code within a one-to-three-mile range.

Chapter 1

The State of Health in the US

Our Physical and Mental Health Begins with Food

D id you know that every time you sneak into the kitchen with a sudden urge for something to eat, statistically, what are you searching for? Something your conscious would say no to? The latest junk food craze, a tiny piece of a forbidden food, a sugar-spiked sweet that you've been desperately craving? What are you imagining right now?

Here's a look at what usually happens when a person walks into a convenience store, a drugstore, or a big-box store to make a purchase. They may enter the store with one thing in mind. What do they usually walk out with? According to research, they walk out the door with a bag filled with processed foods, which may include chips, salsa, spray cheese, a colorful box of cereal, a frozen dinner, a can of soda, a cookie, a candy bar, a donut.

According to marketplace statistics, convenience stores, drugstores, and big-box stores now sell more groceries than traditional grocery stores.[1]

And what is the effect of a shopping bag full of processed foods on our personal health? As William J. McCarthy, adjunct professor in the Fielding School of Public health at UCLA, tells his students, "Highly processed food makes you sick."[2]

If our daily food choices can make a big difference in the state of our health, what about the place where we live, the place we call home?

Does it matter where we live?

Yes. The place where we live matters. A "food desert"[3] is a place where a major grocery store that stocks its shelves with fresh fruits and vegetables is located more than a two-mile walk away from where that person lives. Without adequate public transportation, the only choice someone who lives in a food desert may have is to purchase their food from convenience store, drugstore, liquor store, or fast-food takeout place.

Sixteen communities scattered across Metro Denver, Colorado, are considered food deserts. People who live in these urban communities lack easy access to fresh food and statistically have a higher health risk due to the highly processed food they purchase and consume.

Rural places can be food deserts, too. Native Americans living on reservation land in arid or semi-arid western states may also live in a food desert if the closest major grocery store is more than a 30-minute drive away.

People who live in food deserts typically experience a higher rate of chronic illness, such as diabetes, heart disease, and cancer.

The risk, however, is close to the same for both the person living in a food desert and the urban dweller who has easy access to a major grocery store, when the daily food choices they make are the same.

What people put in their shopping cart makes all the difference when it comes to personal health. Do they fill it with boxes, bags, and cans of processed foods?

Or are the bags they carry out of the store filled with fresh, whole, fiber-rich foods such as soft, soluble fiber-rich vegetables and spinach, kale, box choy, tomatoes, onions, garlic, sweet potatoes, apples, and blueberries, and crunchy carrots, celery, broccoli, and cabbage.

People who frequently chose the convenience of a fast-food meal over fresh food face an even higher health risk. Why?

Fast foods pose an even greater health risk to the communities they serve because these quick, less expensive foods are even more processed than packaged food.[4]

Each choice you make can make a world of difference in increasing your health risk or improving your physical and mental health.

Here is why.

The most recent annual report on the state of health and mental health in the US offers a troubling view of our personal and collective health.[5]

These reports give us a snapshot of where we are right now. However, the message contained in this book and the describing the role of First Food Responders is to show us what we can do better, how to eat better food, and how making the right food choices, over and over, every day, can help get us there.

The annual report states the bad news first: Today, 42 percent American adults are obese, while another 30.7 percent were overweight—nearly 73 percent of adult Americans overall.

Among children and young people between the ages of 2 and 19, 19.3percent are obese, with 6.1percent of kids identified as being severely obese.

In 2013, the average number of prescriptions per person was 12.2 per year. In adults aged 65 to 79, the average was 27.3 prescriptions per year!

By 2021, midway through the COVID-19 pandemic, the number of prescriptions prepared and dispensed to individuals with health problems nationwide had risen to more than 4 billion prescriptions per year.

Take Kentucky, for example. In 2019, Kentucky led the US with 20 retail prescriptions per person, while the national average stood at 11.6 prescriptions per person.[6]

These numbers get even worse for older adults. The average older adult takes four or more prescription drugs each day. And the total is even higher for seniors: 39 percent of seniors take five or more prescriptions each day to treat or manage a specific medical problem. Each prescription comes with its own risks and side effects.

What medical researchers who focus on longevity know is this: The more medications a person takes, the higher their chances are for experiencing adverse reactions, negative side effects, and even life-threatening conditions. The side effects from the simultaneous use of multiple medications in the elderly is a major contributor to disability, frailty, falls, long-term care placement, and a decreased quality of life.

The same holds true for mental health. Up until now, the standard treatment has meant that each patient receives one or more medications and ongoing conversations with a psychiatrist. What has been the effect of that decades-long approach to mental health? In 2021, the American Psychological Association reported that stress in America has now become a national mental health crisis.[7]

Despite this bad news, you might be surprised to learn that along with known mental health benefits from exercise, meditation, yoga, and massage, there's a new kid on the block: soft, soluble, fiber-rich foods can help reverse the health impacts of anxiety, stress, and depression. The first positive results can show up in less than 24 hours.

And there's more good news!

You can take the first steps to lift yourself to a higher level of health and mental well-being every time you reach for something to eat. All it takes is for you to make a conscious choice about what kind of food you eat, each and every time you eat.

Right now, you have the power in your own hands to make a positive change in your personal health and strengthen your mental health, based on the type of food you choose to eat. It's that simple.

When we begin to take charge of the small and large decisions we make every day, especially with the food choices we make, we can set ourselves on the path to better personal health and mental well-being. And we can model this positive change in our health for our friends and family.

While many people choose to reach outside themselves for a quick fix or a solution, you can choose another path. Why reach for an off-the-shelf or prescription drug when your own best pharmacy lies within?

Fresh, local, fiber-rich food prepared in your own kitchen has always been the best medicine. This is true now, and it has always been true throughout our human history.

It wasn't by accident that most of the life-threatening diseases that affect human health and mental health today did not exist 100 years ago.

One hundred years ago, most people lived in small towns and villages across America. Their lifestyle was active, not sedentary, like the lifestyle of many in today's workforce and seniors. People worked on their farms and grew crops and raised livestock.

Prior to World War II modern-day diseases like obesity, heart attack, stress, and colorectal cancer were virtually unknown. Here's why.

At the turn of the century and up until World War II, we were a rural, agricultural country. Seventy percent of America was directly or indirectly involved in agriculture. There were a few big cities on the coasts and in between, but America's heartland was mainly agriculture.

People were physically active outdoors and had easy access to good nutrition, including fresh, chemical-free, fiber-rich fruits and vegetables and meats that had been grown or raised in their own backyard or purchased from a neighbor's small family farm, food stand, or local grocery store.

Due to their active lifestyle and diet that included fiber-rich foods, heart attacks and other modern-day diseases were virtually unknown. The biggest threat prior to 1900 was bacterial infection.

In 1900—almost 29 years before penicillin was discovered—most people wound up with bacterial infections with common names like typhus, typhoid, diphtheria, streptococcus, and staphylococcus, and venereal diseases like syphilis and gonorrhea. These were major diseases before penicillin.

During those years, when a farm family sat down for dinner, the meal often included foods like roast beef, fresh churned butter, and fiber-rich fruits and vegetables. However, over time, the food these farm families ate became more and more processed. The flour used to make pancakes, cakes, and cookies became more and more refined. The lifestyle of the farmer who was able to hire other people to work the field for them became more and more sedentary.

Before World War II, the idea that a person could die from heart disease was so uncommon that when a young medical student by the name of Paul Dudley White decided to study heart disease and become a cardiologist, his fellow medical students laughed at him, telling him: "Paul, you're going to starve, because you're going into a field where so few people have heart attacks!"

However, after the war, in 1953, White became the personal physician and cardiologist to Dwight D. Eisenhower, the 34th president of the United States.

Congestive heart failure became a new, emerging health risk for soldiers who had fought in World War II and were now returning to the workforce.

Eisenhower's time spent in a war zone shows why his health began to fail.

In World War II, Eisenhower was in charge of everything, D-Day operations, all the Allied Forces United Nations, and the whole European Theater of Operations. He was the most well-known person in the world at the time. Everyone loved him.

One of his biggest talents was his ability to get everyone to work together across many cultures. His big smile helped him draw everyone together to work toward a common solution.

During the war years, when Eisenhower was around the age of 54, he had ileitis—inflammation of that part of the small intestine called the ileum. Why would a man of this relatively young age get illeitis?

Eisenhower was basically living in the field with his soldiers. He was eating the same C-rations and K-ration desserts that his soldiers were eating: beef stew, spaghetti and meatballs, mac and cheese, cookies, and chocolate bars.

C-rations and K-rations were processed by design to taste good. The canned and packaged products provided soldiers with a steady diet of ready-to-eat food and a sugary dessert.

Although Eisenhower had access to advice from the best medical doctors in the world, he suffered for the rest of his life from two serious diseases: congestive heart failure and ileitis.

Today few people know that the heart is a muscle. And like any muscle in our body, it needs to be exercised. Aerobic exercise strengthens the heart. This is good. However, Eisenhower's inflamed gut did not make sense until medical science finally discovered that the real cause of his inflamed intestine was the highly processed food he ate during the war years and continued to eat after the war.

The canned food and processed food Eisenhower ate had almost zero fiber.

All the hard and soft fiber found in the vegetables in a can of beef stew had been broken down mechanically, through processing, cooking, and canning.

The fiber in the food he ate had been broken down to the point where it had lost its healing power.

Today, the same thing is true for machine-processed juice drinks and smoothies. Using a machine such as a blender turn our favorite fruits and vegetables into a juice drink or smoothie breaks down the fiber. Fruits and vegetables that are heated or blended to break down the fiber are treated as sugar by the body. And sugar spikes insulin. Over time, the gut becomes inflamed.

Modern-day diseases like chronic heart failure and equally life-threatening health risks linked to inflammation of the gut slowly made their way into modern society after World War II. It took other major diseases related to stress a little longer to make their way into the medical literature.

For example, in 1977, it seemed that no one was suffering from stress. That was the year when the co-author of this book, Joel Rauchwerger, who had been serving on the faculty at Baylor College of Medicine, decided to leave academia and open the doors of the Stress Management Clinic of Houston, Texas. When he registered the name of his new business at City Hall, he was astonished to discovered that he would be the very first person to enter the word *stress* in the Houston, Texas, business directory.

He had received acclaim from the American Association of Retired Persons, more commonly known as AARP, for his book *The Type C Personality: The Cancer Personality*. From his research, Rauchwerger knew a lot about stress and its negative impact on health, and the book had referenced breaking medical reports done in the laboratory where he worked at Baylor.

Rauchwerger had also worked for the world-famous cardiologist Michael DeBakey and served on the medical team for the "boy in the bubble," David Vetter, who was born without any immune system and was placed inside a plastic bubble, where he lived for the next 15 years before dying of cancer.

What research and his book had shown was that long-term stress weakens a person's immune system. To counter this impact, Rauchwerger had developed a training protocol to teach specific stress-relief techniques to his clients, which included biofeedback and eating soft, soluble fiber-rich foods.

A letter of rejection sent by a publisher at the time told him bluntly: "No one today is dying of stress!"

Today, the World Health Organization calls stress the "Health Epidemic of the 21st Century." Stress in the work-places is estimated to cost American businesses $300 billion a year.[8]

Over the past 40 years, thousands of books and training programs have sprung up promising to help people reduce stress. Corporate America, in fact, has become such a lucrative target market for these programs that in 2016 Harvard research report was published titled "The Great Training Robbery." In their report, the three authors pointed their finger directly at the culprit: "In 2012 U.S. corporations spent $164.2 billion on training and education. Over-whelming evidence and experience shows, however, that most companies are unable to transfer employee learning into changes in individual and organization behavior or improved financial performance. Put simply, companies are not getting the return they expect on their investment in training and education. By investing in training that is not likely to yield a good return, senior executives and their HR professionals are complicit in what we have come to call the 'great training robbery.'"[9]

So, if corporate training has not made a dent in reducing stress in the workplace, what does work?

Food, for starters. And our ability to make the right food choices. Today, food rich in both hard fiber and soft, soluble fiber has been recognized as a major player in restoring our physical and mental health and well-being.

The well-documented benefits of fiber-rich foods have created a whole new field of mental health.

Today, around the world, and especially here in the US, many people, and virtually 100 percent of homeless people, experience some type of mental health issue. Yet hardly anyone knows about this new field of mental health or that a whole new field of psychiatry has opened up. The psychiatrists on the leading edge of this new frontier in mental health are studying one thing, and one thing only: the many beneficial chemicals produced by the good bacteria that live in the microbiome, a newly discovered three-pound organ located in our gut. When we feed it its favorite food, the microbiome will produce positive benefits across a wide spectrum on every aspect of our mental health and physical well-being.

The chemicals produced in the microbiome have beneficial effects not only on stress relief, but also on reducing anxiety and depression, which are major mental health problems.

The chemicals produced in the microbiome have a wonderful effect on our mental health and well-being. Their discovery has launched a whole new field of psychiatry called psychobiotics.[10] *Psycho* stands for the brain and *biotic* for the microbiome.

At last, we now know that there is one and only one thing that will produce all these good chemicals, and that is more soft, soluble fiber in the diet.

There are two types of fiber: insoluble fiber and soluble fiber. When you feed the good bacteria in the microbiome its favorite food—soluble fiber—they will crank out a whole natural pharmacy inside of you, a mix of natural chemicals produced by your own body that will help improve and strengthen your own mental health and, by extension, the mental health and well-being of people who follow this path to improved health.

This is one of the main reasons why we designed the training program for our First Food Responders called 23Ingredients.[11]

23Ingredients is a single meal plan that can be created anywhere in the world and is quick and easy to use by people of all ages in all countries and cultures to help improve their health and mental well-being.

Together with local, seasonal food choices, the 23Ingredients menu planner offers the knowledge and guidance needed to help us make the right food choices.

The following story illustrates how just a few simple changes in our daily food choices can make a world of difference in improving our physical and mental health and overall well-being. All it takes is that we just do this.

What if you were given a day off from life as you know it? What if you had one perfect day to do exactly what you wanted to do? That might be your chance to lie your life your way.

Suppose you were given the chance to live free of all obligations to other people; free of other people's expectations. What would you choose to do? What would motivate you to get out of bed that morning? What would put a smile on your face? How would you act? How would you feel?

And would you be thankful? Even joyful? Would your heart be filled to the brim with happiness if you were given a reward each time you took the time to do this one thing first?

Here is what happened when a lawyer, a teacher, and a reporter for a small-town newspaper were each given the opportunity to do this. Can you tell which one did it and what the reward was?

All three people were considered successful by anybody's standards. They all lived in nice houses, drove nice cars, and had enough income to buy what they wanted to eat. They dressed well. They lived the "good life."

The lawyer was known for his wisdom and for the circle of famous men and women who often called or stopped by to talk to him. He found it easy to offer a smile and a hug to others.

The teacher, too, was well known. She was famous for her frequent "calls to action" sent out to her large network of friends, inviting them to join her at some local protest that she firmly believed would help make the world a better place.

And the reporter? He was always on edge, always telling others, "I gotta run. It's chop-chop time!"

Who was the happiest: the lawyer, the teacher, or the reporter?

The lawyer, when asked, would say, "There's no more joy in my life."

The teacher would complain, "I didn't choose to come into this world of suffering."

And the reporter would say, "I'm living the good life!"

What was the reporter doing that made the difference? He was following Mother Nature's number one success strategy. Some call it the Prosperity Principle. It started with a feeling of discomfort that led him to this simple, easy-to-understand rule:

DO THE RIGHT THING

Is that it? Yes!

When you do the right thing, Mother Nature gives you a reward.

She replaces your sense of edginess with a good feeling. You feel good. You might even shout it out: "I'm feeling really good right now!"

It's that simple. Every time you do something right, you get a reward. It comes from the inside out. Some people refer to it as the feel-good feeling that seems to bubble up from their belly, making them want to smile, dance, and laugh out loud.

So, what did they do to feel that good?

They did the right thing. They did a right action. They took a step in the right direction.

Think about it. What do chipmunks, squirrels, and birds have in common? Each day, they have a burning desire to do something; some might call it "being driven by hunger." Whatever the source, it manifests as motivation. They feel motivated to get up and go outside to search for food. When they find it, they get a reward.

So is the reward food? Not exactly. The reward is that good feeling that reminds them they did the right thing. The food that is just right for them is what they eat.

We humans get that very same feeling inside of us. It's part of a two-step reward system that Mother Nature designed to help animals and humans do the right thing, for survival. In the medical journals, it's called the dopamine serotonin reward system. Here is how it works.

In order to ensure that we would survive difficult times outdoors in the elements, Mother Nature gave us a "pharmacy" inside our own body. I guess you could call it a carrot-and-stick reward system.

To motivate us to do the right thing, she gave us a jolt of dopamine that makes us feel edgy and uncomfortable. It reminds us to get up, stand up, move our body, do something, anything, that is life enhancing. Life affirming. That is, do something that has a higher purpose.

That edgy feeling is the first clue that we are on track to getting a reward. So, what do we do next?

- Do we go to the refrigerator and look for the box with that leftover birthday cake from last night?

- Do we call up the pizza place and ask for home delivery?
- Do we light up, drink up, or doll ourselves up to look like a tempting cupcake for someone else's desire?
- Or do we do the right thing?

You know that the last choice is correct. Get up, stand up, move your body, breathe a little deeper. Then we might go further: do some act of compassion, driven by a sense of higher purpose, that returns us—in that moment—to the time when we all lived a lifestyle free of ego, when we lived without separation from nature and all that nourished, sustained, and surrounded us.

A word of caution: While millions of people have discovered how to follow this simple instruction to success, many other people don't really understand the true meaning of the statement "do the right thing."

So, like the lawyer and the teacher, they reach outside of themselves to gain an "off-the-shelf" reward that brings them a feel-good empty reward. Yes, the serotonin will flow and make you feel good for a moment. However, there is nothing life-enhancing in the action you took to gain the reward.

This serotonin pulse that is a part of Mother Nature's original operating system has now been morphed by modern circumstances to serve another purpose. You can use this same dopamine-serotonin reward system to serve a higher cause: to strengthen your immune system and move toward optimum health so that in good health you are able to help serve the needs of others.

While the state of health in the US may have reached an all-time low, the good news is that there has never been in the whole of human history such a series of medical breakthroughs that show us how a series of simple lifestyle and food changes can put us back on the right track toward better health.

What was true at the beginning of time is true today. Mother Nature intended for us not to just survive, but to thrive!

The choice is ours to make.

Chapter 2

Hunger in America Has a New Solution

A Local Network of 1,000 First Food Responders

How many people are going to bed hungry tonight in your community? Where do the elderly, individuals with health issues, hungry children, refugees, and food insecure live? Do any of them live in your neighborhood or in your zip code?

Has your community been identified as a high-risk area for a wildfire, flood, drought, or hurricane? If so, how many residents might be forced to evacuate? If they are displaced and in need of food, who will feed them?

For civic leaders this is both a food security and a logistics problem with a local solution that is staring us in the face. It is a problem that can be solved by creating a countywide network of 1,000 local First Food Responders.

Who are they?

They may be the neighbor next door who loves to cook. Or the person who always shows up at a picnic or a potluck with food you love to eat. It could even be someone in your own family who might be signing up right now to become a First Food Responder.

It could even be you!

Hunger is on the rise in America especially among single women with children and in households that are at or below the poverty level. In year 2 of the COVID-19 pandemic, for example, over 19 million American adults reported that they did not have enough food to eat. This number of people who were experiencing hunger in the US was almost three times the number of people who were identified by the government as food insecure in 2019.

In both groups, those who said they didn't have enough to eat were typically the most vulnerable populations in the US. In addition to those mentioned above, the food insecure also include the elderly, children, and individuals with health issues or a disability.[12]

In addition to these vulnerable Americans, there is another group 13.5 million people who are mostly overlooked and also suffer from hunger. These are the people who live in a rural or urban area that has been identified as a food desert.

What people who live in a food desert have in common is the lack easy access to sources of healthful food.

Although there are many organizations across America that step forward to prepare and deliver meals to people who are food insecure, it was the spike in the number of hungry people during the COVID-19 years that was unusual and gave rise to the First Food Responders (FFR).

In the spring of 2020, 23ZIP received an urgent call from the director of a major government agency in Los Angeles, who told us that Los Angeles County had just shut down 18 organizations that had been feeding the elderly in the county, due to COVID-19 cases in their commercial kitchens.

Could we help?

Our solution of a distributed network of licensed home cooks had caught their attention.

Our vision was to create a network of people who loved to cook, who had a home kitchen, and who lived in the same neighborhood or even the same apartment building as a person who needed to eat better food. We would pay them a stipend, give them a scholarship, and guide them through the licensing and certification process. When trained and licensed they would choose to volunteer their time or be paid to prepare and deliver a fresh, home-cooked meal to a neighbor or a family member.

Over time, these First Food Responders would learn one thing more.

Hunger in America is not just about the people who are food insecure; it is also about the people who eat too much of the wrong kind of food.

Perhaps you know of someone who has a beer belly or is carrying around an extra 90 pounds of fat or more on their body. I'm talking about the 70 percent of Americans who are referred to as overweight or obese.

They may actually be starving—but not for lack of food.

According to the World Health Organization, a person can be hungry because they are underfed or underweight, or over-weight or even obese, and suffer from malnutrition due to a lack of fiber-rich and nutrient-dense foods and a lack an adequate amount of vitamins and minerals.[13]

The body of a person who is as thin as a walking stick, the body of a person with a beer belly, and the body of a person with 90 pounds of excess fat in their breasts, belly, hips, and thighs are actually hungry for food. Real, nutritious food.

As Michael Pollan, the author of *The Omnivore's Dilemma*, once said, "Don't eat anything that your grandmother wouldn't recognize as food." Make that "great-grandmother"!

Americans have found it hard to resist the lure of a restaurant that pulls them in with a low-cost all-you-can-eat spaghetti meal, or the ready-when-you-are pizza takeout places where they can order a single pizza for $9.99 that it can be cut into 24 meal-size slices and has a box so big that it doesn't leave much room for dinner plates on a kitchen table. And perhaps that's the point: All the food and toppings you ordered are on the pizza slice.

The problem in the US today is not just a lack of food, but how much food is thrown away each day.

The food choices most of us are making every day offer little value to a body that was designed to be nourished by fiber-rich, nutrient-dense whole food.

The highly refined, machine-processed grain that makes up 80 percent of the food people eat in the modern world is not what we humans used to eat.[14]

Some people have reached a tipping point where even a single bite of a cookie or sip of a sweet drink will lock down fat burning in their body for 24 to 48 hours.

Food that simply takes up space but offers little of value to our body is also referred to as the standard American diet, or SAD.[15]

So why do so many of us prefer the SAD over healthier foods? Here are four reasons why.

1. The force of culture. Most people refer to what they eat as "food," because that is the way everyone in their family ate when they were young or because everyone in their social group eats that way now that they're adults. They shop in the same stores. They eat in the same restaurants or grab a takeout meal from the same fast-food places.

2. Commercialism. Food that has a long shelf life is marketed and sold to grocery stores. If they don't sell it this month, well, no problem, a customer will buy it next month. The art of creating long-lasting manufactured food has become a science. It can travel the world on a cargo ship and still be edible when the can or box is opened.

3. Addiction. Too much white sugar, high-fructose corn syrup, or any other highly refined food or drink is absorbed too quickly, spikes insulin, and shocks the body. Today we know that anything that spikes insulin will stimulate the pleasure center of our brain, which will then release a pulse of the feel-good chemical serotonin. Serotonin is part of Mother Nature's reward system, which was designed to reward us every time we do the right thing. In this case, we get the reward of feel-good serotonin without the benefit that Mother Nature intended. A sugar high followed by a drop in blood sugar, called the sugar blues, drives us to seek out the same food or drug that gave us a momentary rush of pleasure, again and again.

4. Food deserts. As mentioned, food deserts lack easy access to fresh fruit, vegetables, and other healthy whole food products. The only food available for purchase within a 20-minute walk from home is on the shelves of the local convenience store, drugstore, or liquor store.

Urban Agriculture and the Back-to-the-Land Movement

Many of us know someone who is successfully growing some, if not all, of the food they eat in their own home, community garden, or family farm.

How many of these urban gardeners, "back to the land"[16] folks, and their neighbors who never moved away from the land where they grew up look like they are well-fed?

An even more interesting question might be: How many of these people who we might consider well-fed have a health profile that most of us would envy?

To push the question a little further into a new field of mental health: How many of these well-fed people are waking up each morning with a smile on their face, regardless of circumstances? In fact, if asked, they will tell you that this sense of overall well-being actually makes it easier for them to manage or overcome an unexpected challenge.

Today, we are emerging from a global pandemic. Everyone knows someone who was impacted. Social media is flooded with these stories.

Yet, if we were to take a look back to the last pandemic in the US, 100 years ago, what would we see that is radically different from today?

One hundred years ago, we were mostly a rural country. Seventy percent of the population lived off the land, grew their own produce, raised their own livestock, or were involved in agriculture in some way. We woke up with the sun, ate three square meals a day, and went to bed when it was dark. Lights were turned off in homes and businesses across the country. No one traveled the dark roads at night.

Early travelers who took to the air in the 1950s marveled at arriving at nighttime at their destination, perhaps at an airport in Los Angeles, New York City, London, or Paris, where their airplane flew over a dark landscape until the last few minutes of their flight. The airplane was guided down to the runway by two rows of bright lights.

Today, most people in the US live in major cities. From 50,000 feet above the earth, or from a satellite image, we can see a well-lit world where people are awake and active 24/7. And at any hour of the day or night, in any rural or urban area, many people are awake and eating something. "What's to eat? I'm starving!" they may announce to someone or to no one in particular. Are they?

They may feel hungry, but not for the lack of food.

Hunger in the US had its origin in Europe. It began rather unexpectedly, for two different reasons, in both France and England. Let's start with England first.

The Industrial Revolution began in England, in 1820, in the cities of Manchester and Leeds. These two cities were unique in the world in that they had the brain power, coal, steel, and transportation network—trains and cargo ships— needed to create the Industrial Revolution.

Trains and ships and early versions of assembly lines began to dominate the world in the transportation of products and manufactured goods around the world. Because of a rising demand for these products, huge factories were built, and workers came into urban areas from the countryside to work in the big factories.

It didn't take long for the farm family struggling to make a living on a small plot of land to realize that if they moved from their farm to either Manchester or Leeds, they could get a guaranteed job in a factory.

The great migration from farm fields to industrial cities in England began.

As thousands of workers flowed from the countryside into the cities, they needed to be both housed and fed.

The urgent need to feed the vast number of newly employed factory workers led to the mass production of food.

The message for the factory owners was loud and clear: "We've got to feed 10,000 workers who need to be fed!" And the way to do this, they decided, was to create more and more efficiency in the processing, preparation, and packaging of food.

The foods these captains of industry chose at the time were widely available and could meet this need: wheat, rice, corn, and cereal grains.

The food manufacturers knew that if they could fill up the workers with bread, biscuits, English muffins, and cookies, any processed food that had a long shelf life, they would be able to meet the workers' growing demand for food.

They applied the industrial muscle of the Industrial Revolution to the mass production of food. It became efficient to use big rollers to grind wheat and other cereal grains and pulverize the fiber. This mechanical process enabled meal preparation at a scale large enough and efficient enough to feed thousands of workers.

With processed food, they reasoned, you didn't have to worry about shelf life, food spoilage, or refrigeration.

In short, the new industry of manufacturing highly processed food created food that was basically void of fiber because of the industrial strength of machines that could pulverize massive amounts of grain and turn it into a white powder. The flour used in baking bread could also be used to create hundreds of other baked goods.

The origin of processed food in France began a few decades earlier than the Industrial Revolution in England. It began in 1803 with the start of the Napoleonic Wars.

At the time, Napoleon Bonaparte, a French military, and political leader was getting his 650,000 soldiers ready to fight what became known as the Napoleonic Wars.

Historically, soldiers who marched to a war zone had to live off the food they found along the way. With no other option available, they would simply take the food they needed from the farms they passed along the way.

Napoleon realized that his troops were going to be fighting a war in winter and there would not be enough food to feed them. So, he offered a prize of 25,000 francs to the person who could come up with a solution for how to provide daily meals for his 650,000 soldiers.

A baker came up with a solution: canned goods. In 1815, canned foods were invented, and the baker won the prize money.

By 1820 the baker's invention had created a worldwide demand for food that could be processed, boiled, and sealed in a can.

The demand for processed food in a can reached the American cities of New York and Boston in the 1860s.

In 1865, at the end of the Civil War, the Northern states, including the port cities of New York and Boston, continued to focus on commerce, business, factories, and industrial growth. Like England at the start of the Industrial Revolution, the population of the northern states quickly grew to more than a million people.

The Northern states saw a great wave of immigrants arriving from countries such as Scotland, England, Ireland, Germany, Norway, and Sweden for a guaranteed job.

By contrast, the Southern states, which had been rural, with plantations and enslaved people, was not industrial and did not have a business orientation. The plantations had been self-sufficient. The contrasts at that time, between the North and South, could not have been more stark.

While the North remained a booming industrial society, the South was virtually wiped out by the Civil War. Not only did the South lose many soldiers in the war, but their whole economy was gone.

Many of the young Southern soldiers who were returning home from war found that not only was their family gone, but their family farm was also gone, and food was scarce.

So what did they do? Many of these displaced Southern soldiers, called hobos because they were homeward bound,[17] decided to make a right turn and head west for better opportunities.

The Wild West was opened up by these young guys who were skilled with guns because they had fought in the war. They became the cowboys, outlaws, and buffalo hunters of the legendary Wild West.

When compared to men from the conservative Northeast or Midwest, these young men were tough as nails and wild like stallions. They were daredevils who risked everything to carve out a new life for themselves.

A quick word about food in the Wild West. What did people eat?

Let's start with Texas, where three hundred years earlier, the Spanish had brought three types of animals to the Americas: horses, pigs, and cattle.

Over time, many longhorn cattle had escaped and became wild. They grazed in the wild. So, with the arrival of the Southern soldiers, looking for a new beginning out west, one Texas businessman suddenly came up with a new business idea.

If the South had been economically wiped out, and if the Northern states were experiencing a population explosion, there would be a great need in the North for food.

"America's cities in the East need beef, and the beef is right here in Texas."

But how did a businessman in the 1860s get the cattle from Texas to the Northern states? His idea was straightforward. It went something like this: "If we can get the longhorn cattle from Texas to the start of the railroad line in Kansas, we will make a fortune. Our cattle can supply meat for the growing populations in the Northeast."

And who would bring the Texas longhorn cattle to Kansas? The tough young soldiers from the South who had just arrived on horseback. And this launched the era of the cowboys.

The young men could be hired as cowboys to move a herd of 1,000 cattle 1,000 miles from Texas to Kansas along one of 10 trails. The most famous trail they traveled, and perhaps the one with the fewest obstacles, was called the Chisholm Trail.

What Hollywood didn't talk about when they glamorized the life of the cowboy in their movies, was the stark life of the lone cowboy. In reality, the cowboy faced many hardships as he guided a herd of cattle to the railhead in Kansas City.

One of the biggest problems the cowboys faced was insects. They were the target of insects night and day.

Then, during the daytime, as the cowboys drove 1,000 cattle up the trail in front of them, they had to cover their own face with a bandana because of the dust kicked up by the feet of the cattle. The air the cowboys breathed was almost always filled with dust, and some of it ended up in their lungs. So, using the bandana helped protect their lungs from the dust, but it didn't block everything.

If that was not enough, the cowboys quickly realized that cattle are herd animals. That is, if one of the 1,000 cattle gets spooked, they run off in all directions. So how do you wheel them back into a herd? On the trail from Texas to Kansas, a lot of cowboys got trampled in a stampede of cattle.

And then there was the money that cattle represented.

To an outlaw, the beef on those hooves represented big money if they could grab a few cattle on the run. The prospect of easy money attracted many outlaws who would threaten the cowboys and their herd. The choice for the cowboy was stark. A gunfight or a cattle stampede. The sound of a gun could trigger both.

Life became a long, stressful odyssey of endurance for the cowboys.

And then, as suddenly as it started, the 30-year era of the cowboy came to an end.[18]

The reason? Ask a farmer.

Along each of the 10 trails were the croplands of farmers, who didn't use their anger to shoot at the cowboys or cattle who were destroying their farm crops. Instead, they used their intellect to apply pressure on politicians to establish laws to end the cattle drives.

And then, surprisingly, it was not the law but a simple invention that put a sudden end to the cattle drives. At home in their own kitchen, a farmer and his wife took some cheap wire that they had purchased from a hardware store and twisted little barbs along the wire that could prick a finger and cause it to bleed if touched.

The farmer and his wife surrounded their farm with the barbed wire they had created. To their delight and amazement, it worked! The tiny pricks of thousands of tiny barbs twisted into the wire discouraged the cattle from traveling through their farmland. The cattle were deterred by the barbed wire and quickly learned not to go near it.

The farmer's crops were saved. The trails where the cowboys had moved the cattle north from Texas to Kansas were now blocked at various points along the trail by barbed wire that enclosed farmers' land and crops.

The solution? A railroad line was extended south from Kansas to Texas. It provided an easy way for the businessman to bring his cattle to the local railyards. There was no longer a need for cowboys to drive the cattle north to Kansas. Within 10 years, the era of the cowboy was over.

In addition to beef, the Americas were also home to another important food crop.

Corn originated with the Aztecs in Mexico. Easy to plant and harvest, corn spread far and wide, up into California, Arizona, and Colorado and then eastward to the American South. Corn became a staple food of the American South and Southwest.

Corn as a crop also made its way northward to the home of the indigenous Iroquois, Mohawks, Oneida, and Seneca, who considered corn as one of the crops they ate called "three sisters": corn, squash, and beans.

With food preparation in mind, it is important to mention that America's indigenous people never got the deadly disease related to processed corn called pellagra, which is related to the lack of vitamin B3, also known as niacin, in the diet.19 Pellagra is also referred to as the disease of the four Ds: dermatitis, diarrhea, dementia, and death. How did they avoid this disease? Because of the way they prepared the corn.

To soften the corn in preparation for a meal, they soaked it in lye, a mixture of water and wood ash. By soaking the corn to soften it and not boiling it, they preserved the vitamin B3 and thus avoided pellagra.

Many years later, scientists discovered that when corn was softened in lye, it created a previously unknown chemical reaction that softened the corn, which make it easy to eat, and retained the vitamin B3. The vitamin B3 was also retained by using the heat from the midday sun to dry the softened corn, and then hand-grinding it between two stones to turn it into cornmeal for making tortillas.

By contrast, in the American South, almost everyone got a touch of pellagra because they prepared the corn a different way: They boiled the corn, let it dry, and turned it into a coarse powder which felt gritty on the tongue, as in hominy grits.

Scrambled eggs with a side of hominy grits became a popular meal in the South. Blackstrap molasses, beans, and fatback (bacon), and hominy grits made from boiled corn was the standard diet of many people in the American South.

However, the way they prepared the corn, by boiling it to soften it, came with a major health risk that wasn't understood until 1935.

That was the year that a medical team from the US National Institutes of Health, led by Joseph Goldberger, had just ended a two-year study. The medical team had been trying to understand why so many people in the American South were dying of pellagra. The first thought was that these people must be dying from an infectious disease.

Finally, in 1932, Goldberger said, "Wait a second, maybe pellagra is not caused by a bug. Maybe the cause is nutritional."

Goldberger got permission to go to the local jail and ask 10 men if they wanted to participate in a food experiment that would get them out of jail. The ten men agreed and were divided into two groups.

The first group of five men were served freshly prepared meat, vegetables, fruit, and dairy products every day.

The other five men were kept on the standard Southern diet. By the time the experiment ended, each of these five men exhibited the disease pellagra. The cause of pellagra in their diet? The lack of vitamin B3, because it had been killed by boiling the corn.

The best food for this group of men to return them to good health quickly became obvious. It had to be freshly prepared meat, vegetables, fruit, and dairy products.

After learning of the discovery that the lack of vitamin B3 was the cause of the deadly pellagra, the Canadian biochemist, physician, and psychiatrist Abram Hoffer reached out to the American chemist Linus Pauling, who had discovered and popularized the health benefits of vitamin C. The two doctors decided to collaborate on another experiment. They invited 100 patients who had been diagnosed with schizophrenia to participate in an experiment in which they received massive doses of vitamin B3 each day. And it was successful. One out of every three patients was cured.

The success of the experiment showed that one way to help prevent schizophrenia was to include vitamin B3 in the diet.

Look to the Past for Solutions for the Future

Two giant worlds that everyone is interested in are the world of food, because everyone has to eat, and the world of drugs.

The common denominator in both worlds is that you are on the safest ground if you just stick with the whole food as designed by Mother Nature.

In both worlds, the problem lies in refining the food or in extracting and concentrating one of its ingredients. Over a sweep of hundreds of years, the refining of food into powder and extracting certain chemicals from food to concentrate them for use as a drug were technology driven.

This practice of refining food was used even almost 400 years ago. The contrast between the dark, whole grain food the peasants ate and the cakes and pastries made with highly processed white flour that was enjoyed by the aristocrats led to an uprising of the peasants against the French monarchy. Here's why.

At the time of the French Revolution of 1789, the king was Louis XVI and the queen was Marie Antoinette. At that time, the country had experienced a bad harvest. A lot of people living on farms and the women who were working in the fields were starving.

By contrast, many of the French aristocracy, who were living at the Palace of Versailles at that time, were living an extravagant life. The opulent lifestyle of the aristocracy created resentment among the peasants.

Soon, the starving women in the fields started protesting because the difference between the two lifestyles was like night and day.

Marie Antionette's response when told that the peasants had no bread to eat was purportedly "Well, let them eat cake."

It was a flippant remark that only an aristocrat might say. Because the peasants didn't have any bread and because the highly processed white flour to make pastries and cakes was unavailable to them, the peasants became envious. It became a tipping point for revolution.

What neither the aristocracy nor the starving peasants knew at the time was that thick, dark, whole grain bread was much better than the white bread and sweet, fluffy pastries that the nobility were eating.[20]

Today, we know that a loaf of dark bread, which has the bran, the flour, the inner brown husk with the B vitamins, the germ of the plant and its protein, the good fatty acids, and the good vitamin E is a much better choice for a meal if the goal is to maintain good health.

So, the paradox is that the outcry from the women in the fields that sparked the French Revolution was that when bread was available, they were eating the more nutritious bread. The bread was dark in color because it wasn't refined.

Fast-forward to today, and think of how many cookies, donuts, pies, cakes, croissants, refined cereals, and biscotti are eaten every day in the US. How much of a family's food budget is spent on these sweet treats that fill us up with empty calories?

It's all economics. With billions of tons of white flour produced every year in America's heartland, the food manufacturers are going to continuously find other uses for it, like putting it into soups, salad dressing, and more, for purely economic reasons.

It all harkens back to Mother Nature. Our digestive system is designed for fiber, fiber, fiber. That is, food should be crude, like dark, unprocessed bread—dark rye, dark pumpernickel—not processed or refined.

Keep the food you eat whole. The same is true for drugs.

Any plant that has been highly refined to make its addictive chemical stronger and stronger, sometimes as much as 1,500 percent stronger than the original plant, messes up the human brain.[21] It destroys brain cells.

The same is true with alcohol.[22] Around the world, almost every culture around the world has alcohol. If you have a little natural fermentation from yeast, or a natural fermentation from wine or beer, it does not become a serious problem, because the alcohol will kill the yeast at a certain concentration, like 6 percent. In addition, a small amount of beer and wine contain helper factors, like the resveratrol in wine, a few sips of which can stimulate our digestive juices before a meal.

However, when a person or a business distills the alcohol, boils off the alcohol, concentrates it, and then sells it as a hard liquor—bourbon, whiskey, rum, rye, scotch—the result is a refined and concentrated drink that creates a health risk. The risk lies not only in intoxication; alcohol can also damage your liver and etch away at the lining of your gut, which can lead to leaky gut and autoimmune disease.

In France, children are allowed to have a little sip of wine. Wine is left on the table. In small amounts, there is no problem. But once you distill it, you have messed around with Mother Nature. And with concentration comes addiction.

The more you refine food, blend it, boil it, juice it, and break down the fiber into nanoparticles that will be absorbed too quickly by the body and spike insulin, the more addictive it becomes. This is because it is absorbed too quickly and triggers a reaction in the pleasure center of the brain too fast.

This is why sugary food and food made with highly refined flour is referred to as comfort food. It is comforting because it will trigger a pulse of feel-good serotonin because of the addictive quality of the food or the drug.

When we take a look at all of the animals in nature, what are they doing? The squirrels are eating whole foods: nuts, seeds, and whole grain. They are eating foods that are rich in oils, protein, vitamins, and minerals.

Wild animals do not have the technology to refine their food. And look at their energy. Look at the power expressed in the movement of a deer, a bear, a squirrel, or even a bird in flight.

They're following Mother Nature. They're doing exactly as they were designed.

When we look at animals in nature, we are looking at our own potential to achieve similar levels of high energy and inner power.

When we create a series of tiny, positive, life-affirming habits that become part of our daily routine, we will begin to feel our body responding in a positive way. Every day, in every way, we will feel better and better. Every day we will grow stronger and stronger. And every day, we will also grow smarter.

"At 100, I have a mind that is superior—thanks to experience—than when I was 20," Rita Levi-Montalcini told an audience of well-wishers at her 100th birthday party.[23] Back in 1986, she had been awarded the Nobel Prize for a medical breakthrough in the field of physiology that showed how our brain is able to grow new brain cells at any age. She was living proof of this.

Chapter 3

The Homeless Problem in the US

I n 1995, at the beginning of the internet boom, Votelink, one of the first electronic democracy systems on the Internet, began to track timely news events in 10 major cities across the US. Each day, a hot topic would be selected for each city and posted online. "Netizens" would then be invited to vote and comment on the topic. They could vote as many times as they wanted; however, only their last vote counted.

One day, the hottest issue being discussed was the same in each of three different cities: Seattle, San Francisco, and San Jose. That topic was homelessness. Each city had taken an entirely different approach to handling the homelessness problem.

In Seattle, for example, homeless people were being put on city buses and taken to the edge of Kings County, to the end of the bus line. This left the impression that Seattle's fix for their homelessness problem was "Anywhere but here."

In San Francisco, homeless people had been illegally camping in Golden Gate Park. The city had ignored their campsites for some time. Finally, the decision was made to dismantle the campsites. As the local newspapers reported at the time, police, mounted on horseback, had driven the homeless people out of the park. Where did these people go? Perhaps some traveled southward from San Francisco to San Jose.

San Jose, located an hour south of San Francisco and only 12 miles southeast of Silicon Valley, had chosen a different strategy for managing their homelessness problem. San Jose leaders decided to put out a welcome mat for homeless people by converting numerous abandoned warehouses in an economically distressed area of the city into affordable housing.

The housing, they reasoned, would provide a new home for a future Silicon Valley workforce as well as their own local businesses. The construction project would provide immediate jobs that would help ensure a future economic recovery for a distressed area of the city.

Some of the formerly homeless people who found a new home in the city-funded housing may have even filled out job applications and been hired by tech startups such as Facebook, Google, Apple, and Yahoo.

Today, finding a temporary home in transitional housing in a forward-thinking city may also lead to a workforce development program such as First Food Responders, a job that gives them enough money to pay their rent and bills, and food security.

Whether the job is home-based, in an office, or on a job site, the end goal for a formerly homeless person is permanent housing and a job that gives them a sense of purpose, perhaps even a chance to help make the world a better place. What most homeless people want, if asked, is a job that comes with a sense of dignity and respect. Even better is a job that allows them to express their natural skills and talents.

This is a vision that may seem hard for homeless people to imagine if they have lost their sense of hope.

The challenges faced by homeless people and by almost every community seeking an innovative, long-term solution are radically different from the problems they faced 30 years ago. It is also different from the homelessness problem that other countries around the globe face, where the number of displaced and homeless people may reflect a steady stream of refugees fleeing a war zone.

According to a UN-Habitat report, globally, on any given night, more than 1.6 billion people are experiencing homelessness somewhere in the world.[24] With the COVID-19 pandemic, that number has continued to grow.

In 2020, an estimated 580,466 people the US[25] were experiencing homelessness.

Today, we know that the homelessness problem in the US is reaching a crisis point. And we also know at some level—call it gut level—that it doesn't have to be this way.

When we come together to solve a common problem, when we look at what works and what is possible, the entrepreneurial "can do" spirit of America has the capacity to enable us to innovate our way to a positive solution for the benefit of all concerned.

Where there is an alignment of ideas, there is hope for a positive solution. Where there is peace of mind, there is hope for peace in the world.

Most of us share the same dreams and aspirations. Most of us want more peace, love, and harmony in our lives. Most of us share a common compassion for those who suffer. In fact, this compassion for life—all life on Earth—draws us together like a gravitational force for the common good.

So, how is the homelessness problem the US faces today radically different from the one the country faced 30 years ago? The difference shows up in our food, drugs, and lifestyle.

Over the last century, technology has continuously gotten better and better at manufacturing, processing, and refining everything.

Food, which used to be nutrient-rich, has now been processed and refined to the point that foods manufactured and processed at industrial scale may now be nutrient-sparse and addictive. When these foods evoke an inflammatory response or lead to leaky gut, they can also put us at risk of a number of 100 different diseases.

Today in the US, many homeless people who go to sleep at night on a city sidewalk, in a vacant lot, or in a city park are addicted to highly processed foods and fast food. If they have a health issue such as obesity, type 2 diabetes, Alzheimer's disease, high blood pressure, or heart disease, they may also lack easy access to healthcare or a hospital.

Today, nearly 100 percent of homeless people in the US have some type of mental health issue related to stress, anxiety, or depression.[26]

That is perhaps why it may become easy for them to say yes when offered a smoke, an alcoholic beverage, or a drug that over time becomes addictive, because it offers them a moment's relief from the mean streets, the hard times, the social isolation from people passing by, and an anxiety-ridden 24-hour-day with nothing for them to do.

Most people don't realize that some of today's most addictive drugs are up to 1,500 times as potent as those that were available 30 years ago. Drugs that light up the pleasure center of the brain make the drug user instantly feel good. However, when drug use becomes addictive, it messes up the brain, destroys brain cells, and can lead to disruptive, violent, or dangerous behavior.

Over the past 30 to 40 years, major pharmaceutical companies have continued to refine, process, and produce ever more powerful drugs to sell to doctors and pharmacies for public use. Many of these drugs come with a major health risk as a side effect. One of these side effects may include addiction. Companies have made billions of dollars from the sale of addictive drugs to an anxious public, and their success is also reflected at a smaller scale by legal and illegal drug makers and drug dealers who find a highly receptive market for their products among homeless people. Like others in the drug business, they start by offering a free sample.

The third major reason that the problem of homeless in the US today is different from 100 years ago is that most modern technology has now reached a tipping point where its growth is exponential. Technology combined with artificial intelligence is now being integrated into almost every aspect of modern society.

It is now second nature for many of us to turn to technology first for the answer to a question instead of talking to each other or an expert or turning within.

In whom do we trust?

The bottom line is that humans are social creatures. We are capable of self-healing and we have intuition, faith in a higher power, fire in the belly, and that gut feeling that can inform the next decision we make.

We humans enjoy connecting with people in our community. We love the social engagement that enables us to meet socially with others, talk with them, laugh with them, take a walk in nature with them, and marvel together at the wonders of the natural world.

In the distant past, when humans first perfected the art of toolmaking for use in hunting and preparing food, they didn't realize that they were taking the first steps down the road to a future where technology would define and dominate almost every aspect our daily life and lifestyle.

This transition into the addictive quality of modern technology was depicted in a hand-sketched cartoon printed in a local newspaper in 2010. In the cartoon, a young boy is at home, in his bedroom, playing a video game on a desktop computer. The door is help open by his mother, who is calling out to him: "Johnny, it's time for you to go outside and play." The boy responds, "I will, if you buy me a laptop."

Today, the boy's response might be "OK. I will play outside if you buy me a smartphone."

Facebook has imagined its future Metaverse, a world where everyone lives in a virtual world.[27] It's a technology dreamworld where users can imagine and create anything they want, destroy it, and start again. Perhaps it will become a world in which war becomes a game, where no one really gets killed, and at the end of the day everyone unplugs from the computer, has something to eat, and then puts on a headset and is lulled to sleep electronically.

Experts in land and water management of parkland, open space, fish, and wildlife have a straightforward warning for this technology-addicted generation: If you don't value it, you won't protect it.[28]

Another stark reality that is a little closer to home is that when it becomes easier and easier for technology to take up more and more of our children's lives and captivate our own life up to the point of addiction, we then risk breaking the natural human bonds that bind us together.[29]

We also risk losing interest in the real world and a desire to protect it. If a better place is always "out there" someplace else, then we may no longer have a desire to be stewards of the Earth and all its creatures, large and small.

The personal risk to those who prefer immersing themselves in technology to the point where they begin to disengage from the natural world and from each other is that they may lose the natural built-in resilience that most people have that can help them overcome a personal challenge. They may lose the capacity to adapt to rapid change and may destroy the very structure they live in or have no plan B to turn to when there is a power outage.

The phrase *grow or die* becomes meaningless in a life lived in a virtual world where everything can be broken down and rebuilt.[30]

A homeless person addicted to highly processed foods, drugs, or technology may have lost both their resiliency and their ability to adapt. In the process, they may have also disconnected from everything that can offer them hope and a pathway forward.

Homeless people may feel like victims of something larger than themselves. They may feel like easy prey in a world that may seem more and more fearsome to them every day.

There was once a time when fear was essential to human survival. We lived in fear of the saber-toothed tiger and other unseen wild beasts in the forest and took precautions to protect ourselves and our family.

For 99.9 percent of human history, we lived outdoors in nature. We may have been hungry, and we may have been fearful, but we were not homeless.

The sky was our roof, and the earth was our floor. Conditions were harsh. When it rained, we got wet. When it snowed, we got cold. Survival was constantly on our minds.

And there was never enough food. One could say that the mantra of the day was *food-food-food*. Food was everything. Food meant survival. Food was life itself.

At that time in our history, the profession of humans was to hunt and gather food. In fact, if there had been two job listings posted at that time, here is what they might asked for:

> **Wanted:** One Hunter-Gatherer. Must be able to run 20 miles or more and grapple with wild animals.
>
> **Wanted:** Someone to gather food, including plants and seeds, prepare meals, and ensure the survival of the children.

These were skills that required great courage, for at any moment, our nomadic ancestors had to also meet the random challenges of weather, hostile clans, and perhaps a wild animal running through the community or pursuing them as food.

The job of the hunter required special skills. The hunter needed to work well with a team. They had to be willing travel far away from home, stay on the same wavelength, and stay focused on the same goal. They need to be able to follow the prey, kill it, and then carry it home.

For many of them, the capture of food was no easy task. Research has shown the some of these hunters may have may have suffered as many broken bones as a modern day rodeo rider.

For others, activities centered around the children and their community. They had a love of the environment that sustained them.

And then, seemingly overnight, our human lifestyle changed. The Agricultural Revolution changed everything.

Overnight, we went from an active, nomadic lifestyle to a sedentary lifestyle. Our daily job shifted from a constant search for food to harvesting an abundance of grain and the domestication of animals.

No longer nomadic, our ancestors settled down in areas where the soil was rich and there was plenty of water for irrigation. In these areas of rich soil, water, and abundant food, villages grew into towns, and towns grew into cities.

This stability, and the ability to set down roots in a single location, resulted in a population explosion.

Along with a lifespan that had expanded to 75 years, the number of children in a family grew from one or two to 12 or more. The farms needed farmhands. The children were given chores around the house and the farm as soon as they were able.

There was an abundance of food right outside their door. There was also a destruction of the environment.

For the first time in human history, there was private property, water rights, law and order, and the creation of cities. For the first time, legal systems, jails, and bureaucracies were established to manage the growing complexity of an ever-larger population.

Overnight, we shifted from a very simple lifestyle around the fire or the hearth to the development of communities, the management of ever larger groups of people, and the complexity of integrating diverse lifestyles and social customs into a unified, peaceful, and productive community where everyone had a place they could call home and a job.

America in the mid-1800s also faced a similar influx of thousands of families arriving from Ireland at the port cities of New York and Boston.

Due to a famine in their country, many of the Irish came to the United States to find a job. Instead of a warm welcome, they were greeted with a warning sign that read "If you're Irish, don't apply." How did the Irish overcome this challenge, find a job to support their family, and integrate into society? With numbers on their side, they chose the most charismatic leaders in their community and elected them to public office. Once in office, these leaders created jobs for the Irish in the local police force. Today, across the US, Americans celebrate the Irish every March 17 with a St. Patrick's Day parade.

Times change. We live at a time of rapid change. Those who can stay flexible and adapt to rapid change set the pace for others to follow.

In 1943, American psychologist Abraham Maslow popularized the idea that the three most basic needs of humans were food, clothing, and shelter.

Eighty years later, it's time for Maslow's hierarchy of needs to be updated to include Parkinomics, which states that the most basic needs of modern humans are food, clothing, shelter, and a job.[31]

It's important to realize that one of 12 major causes of homelessness in the US is unemployment or underemployment,[32] whereby an individual or family does not have a job or make enough money to pay their bills.

It's not exactly a job that is the problem. It's the type of job that is being offered.

Right now, there are more jobs available than people applying for them. How many of these jobs are considered bad jobs, the kind that most people won't go near?

What constitutes a good job? A job that pays a living wage. A job that comes with dignity and respect. A job that is home-based, perhaps nontechnical, so that if they choose, they can work from home and take care of their children or be a caregiver to a family member.

If you have a home kitchen and love to cook, you can now make enough money to pay your bills by preparing and delivering meals to the food insecure.

Another major cause of homelessness is population displacement due to climate impacts.

Climate impacts can happen anywhere within the span of a few minutes or days and turn the lives and livelihoods of hundreds or thousands of people upside down.

In an instant, people who had been going about their daily lives can suddenly be displaced, disoriented, and distraught.

At a peak moment of a climate impact, a displaced person may panic. They may make a poor decision or a decision they may regret later. They may become disoriented, experience PDSD, and become unable to make the right decision.

This mental disorientation may last for months. Unable to cope with the stress of a life changing situation, a displaced person may ultimately turn to drugs as an aid to reduce anxiety, stress, or depression. They may become addicted to prescribed drugs, which may ultimately lead them to homelessness.

While many people may have the resilience or coping skills that enable them bounce back when everything around them has been destroyed, others are not so resilient. They may have lost their resilience because the climate event that drove them from their home may have happened once or twice before. A person living in a tornado zone in Kentucky returns to rebuild their home in the same location after it was destroyed. A person returns to a home destroyed by flooding or a wildfire and rebuilds a strong home, up to modern building standards, only to see it lost again in another climate disaster.

In 2021, the National Oceanic and Atmospheric Administration reported that there were 20 separate billion-dollar climate disasters across the US that year.[33] It was the third costliest extreme weather year on record and tested the limits of community and human resilience from coast to coast. The report included predictable tornadoes, hurricanes, cyclones, ice, and flooding that year after year disrupt or destroy homes, croplands, and communities across the heartland of the US. Year after year, the storms return, again and again, and a 20-foot surge of water knocks down homes and businesses that have been built and rebuilt along the coastline.

Some climate impacts that displace thousands of people could not have been predicted in the past. The Marshall Fire, which destroyed 1,000 homes in Colorado in only a few hours the day before New Year's Eve 2022, happened in the middle of winter.

Two days later, five inches of snow covered all signs of loss and devastation.

There had been a drought in Colorado, but prior to that time, fire season was not year-round. The wind-driven wildfire displaced 30,000 people.

Something else had not been predicted. The fire had knocked out all the electricity in the area. All house lights, streetlights, and, perhaps most important, gas station pumps—which rely on electricity to recharge an electric vehicle or pump gas into cars and trucks—were inoperable.

Those who didn't have enough fuel in their car to leave town ended up at an emergency shelter along with other residents who relied on public transportation or a bicycle to get around town and were unable to find a way to evacuate.

These sudden climate impacts and the destruction of what has come to define us—food security, housing security, and our material goods and family treasures—make us feel vulnerable.

There is no map in our head or hands for the unknown territory or challenges that lie ahead. There is little resilience left for some people to continue to return and rebuild in places that are predictably known to have a similar climate event return the next year, or the year after.

For some people, this becomes a breaking point. For others, it becomes a starting point for testing their ability to survive, adapt, and even thrive. As the saying goes, what doesn't kill us makes us stronger.

In addition to unemployment or underemployment, what are other primary root causes of homelessness in America?[34]

- Stagnant wages
- Lack of affordable housing
- Lack of affordable healthcare
- Poverty
- Lack of mental health and addiction treatment services
- Racial inequality
- Domestic violence
- Family conflict
- Systemic failures

For those of us who know someone who has become homeless or see them struggling to survive another day on the streets, the following stories may restore the resilience, faith, and strength needed for someone who has lost their way to find their way home again.[35]

The Astronaut

Earth to Astronaut: You may have aimed too high and over-shot the moon. Maybe your goals were too big. You are now heading back to Earth. Along the way, you may have lost any sense of the mission or money you were pursuing. You may have also lost your baggage. You are now streamlined for the long fight home.

Right now, you are reentering the Earth's atmosphere as naked as a newborn. All past labels have been burned off on reentry. It is a perfect time for you to reinvent yourself. This is a good thing. It's also a good time to redefine your relationship to money.

The High Diver

Lifeguard to High Diver: You may have suffered a sudden loss of your job, your steady income, and your company-sponsored healthcare. I'm here to tell you that everything is OK. You will be able to adjust. It's your choice. There is still water in the pool. Go ahead and dive in.

You know how to swim, right? If not, I have included some swimming instructions, and a few thoughts to hold in mind as you let go, push off, and free-fall into the water.

High Diver, will you land in a pool of cold water? Or is your pool in a river that will carry you to the sea? Could your pool be filled with hand squeezed lemonade, made by your caring friends? Or is it perhaps a money pool? Will you dry yourself off only to discover that your skin carries a sheen of gold? What are you thinking as you dive off the board?

The Flat-Tire Crowd

Bike Racer to Novice: You've got the bike. You've got the job. You're holding on tight to what you have. Yet with two tires flat, there is no place to go. In this economy, you may think that you are stuck in the job you have right now.

If you are a risk taker, you could walk away, take the Metro, or fix those flat tires yourself. If you are ready for change—and continuously reinventing yourself is the game—read on. I have given you some new strategies to think about in your spare time.

In the meantime, use the money you are making to pay down your bills. Contribute to charity. Now is not the time to invest wildly. It is not PC nor beneficial to your future.

The Apprentice

Teacher to Student: It is time to get up out of that chair and get physical. Your family may have lost that nest egg that they were saving to pay for your education. You may have been unable to find a scholarship or loan to help you jump over the wall and into vocational school, college, or university.

As a student, you are luckier than most, because there are so many options still available to you. You will need to drop all expectations and take another look at the road ahead. You don't have to move forward stuck in first gear. So breathe a sigh of relief. Life is an open book; you can be one of its best students if you start today.

The Inlander

Inner Guide to Outer Self: Your health challenge may make you feel as though life has turned upside down. I feel deep compassion for you and your health situation.

Right now, your health is your number one focus. It's time to turn inward. If someone were asked to list the most important things in their life, money would not be at the top of their list.

First on the list would be good health, perhaps even perfect health. Next comes love of family and friends. Happiness is number 3.

Money turns up fourth, and even then, it is couched in words that include wealth, well-being, abundance, and beauty. A walk in nature can give you this for free.

The Bystander

City to Citizens: If you are newly homeless, we can help you move off the streets into safe housing. If the temporary housing does not include a kitchen, we will hire an organization to provide you with fresh, healthy food. There are also family shelters and transitional housing. For us to find you, you must first reach out to us.

If you can be a quiet, respectful neighbor and live free of drugs and alcohol, we will work to find a place for you in a community where you can thrive. In community, you will be able to engage in a set of daily activities and learn new, healthy habits that will help you rebuild your physical health and strengthen your mental health. This positive habit formation will enable you to return to the workforce with a job that helps you express your own natural talents and skills. It will be a job that provides you with dignity and respect and offers you a chance to become a productive member of the community. This is our goal. We hope it is also your goal.

Chapter 4

Supply Chain and Distribution

Disruption, Innovation, and Timely Solutions

The Origins of the Supply Chain

H uman health is based on variety of foods, including fiber-rich foods, not just the monoculture of grains such as wheat, barley, oats, and rice that have become dominant in our diet with the rise of the Agricultural Revolution.

When grain products became the primary foundation of the human diet, anthropologists who did research on the food our ancestors ate were able to distinguish between those people who were born after the start of the Agricultural Revolution and those who were nomadic and born before its start, based on their skeletons.

The skeletons of people whose daily meals were based on grains were, on average one foot shorter than their nomadic ancestors. Their joints showed signs of arthritis, their bones have a lot less calcium, and their teeth were replete with dental cavities.

By contrast, the skeletons of their nomadic ancestors who had lived off the land and whose diets were about 70 percent fiber were just the opposite. Their bones and teeth were strong. Did you know that bones are 95 percent protein and only 5 percent calcium? This discovery underscored the reason that the nomads were also one foot taller: fish from rivers and the ocean, eggs taken from bird nests, and protein from meat. The accidental discovery that cooked meat tasted better than raw and was easier to digest helped the human brain grow larger to its present weight of about three pounds.

Some historians have called the Agricultural Revolution the biggest mistake humanity has ever made in terms of a loss of health, the stratification of societies into rich and poor, and in the conflicts that led to war based on the wealth of those who controlled the supply and distribution of grain.[36]

Imagine, for example, the wealth of the landholders who were able to grow and deliver the tons and tons of grain that was required to feed the millions of laborers who built the Egyptian pyramids.

Imagine the wealth of landowners in Sumeria, which included Babylon and what we know as modern-day Iraq, who were able to supply millions of tons of grain that were needed to feed the laborers who were put to work building the ancient structures called ziggurats, where each step up to the top—which was flat—was smaller than the one below it.

The building of the ziggurats required so much distribution of food to the laborers that most historians agree that a demand for accounting of where the food was being distributed led to the origin of writing on cuneiform tablets.[37]

In Peru, massive agriculture, which included potatoes and other root crops, was required to feed the workers who built Machu Picchu, the royal estate of Incan emperor Pachacuti. The building of the emperor's estate began around 1450 CE, and it ceased functioning about ninety years later, when the Spanish conquistadors arrived and the Inca Empire was destroyed.

The Supply Chain of the Roman Empire

Remember the phrase *all roads lead to Rome*? What does it mean? The Roman Empire as it was known between 500 BCE and 500 CE was vast. The land that Rome controlled formed a ring around the Mediterranean Sea and included what we now refer to as Portugal, Spain, France, Italy, Greece, Morocco, Algeria, Tunisia, Liberia, Egypt, Palestine, and modern-day Israel.

Rome was all business and commerce. Roads were built and maintained in good repair to facilitate both business and military movements. In those days, when all roads did lead to Rome, silk came from China, grain came from Egypt, and a unique purple dye produced by the Phoenicians that came to be associated with power and wealth because it was expensive and complex to produce came from the region now called Lebanon.

The "royal purple" dye was produced from the secretions of snails.[38] It was greatly valued as a dye for cloth that could be turned into robes because the color did not easily fade. Instead weathering and sunlight actually made it brighter.

This trade to and from the Middle East along the roads that were built and maintained by Rome continued for many years, until Rome fell into the hands of invaders.[39] Suddenly, almost all business and commerce to and from Europe ceased. Why?

Because the roads built during the rise of the Roman Empire fell into disrepair. In addition, travel to faraway places over rough roads made those brave travelers who did travel from home an easy target for robbers. The farthest distance the average European farmer traveled away from home in a lifetime was only 10 miles.

The Crusaders' Supply Chain

The supply chain that had kept goods and services moving throughout the Roman Empire but had been disrupted after the fall of Rome got an unexpected boost from a series of nine Crusades to the Holy Lands. The Crusades last for a period of about 200 years despite the rough condition of the roads and the ever-present risk of robbery.

The Crusades, which began around 900 CE, had begun with a proclamation from Pope Urban II that basically said,

"Hey, you can redeem yourself from all of the sins you committed in the past. You can wipe out all of those sins if you go on a crusade to the Holy Lands and liberate Jerusalem from the Infidels."[40]

The Crusaders who traveled to the Middle East from Europe were exposed to two major commodities that, at that time, were only available from the Middle East: spices and sweet sugary food in all of its forms and varieties. Sugar and spices to that point were unknown to Europeans.

When the Crusaders returned home, they brought the spices and sugary confections with them. Europeans' daily meal at that time comprised a porridge made out of wheat, barley, and oats; perhaps a little beer made from barley; and root crops like turnips. The addition of spices and sugary foods to that meal was like a drug.

Demand in Western Europe began to grow. It didn't take long for the entrepreneurs of the time to realize they could make a lot of money by importing spices and sugary sweets from the Middle East.

With rising demand came the rise of businessmen who were willing to make the dangerous trip to the Middle East to purchase spices and sugary foods and bring them back to Europe.

The Silk Road Supply Chain

In 1200 CE, a 17-year-old Venetian named Marco Polo set out on a business and adventure trip with his father and uncle to the court of Kublai Khan, the emperor of China.

Kublai also happened to be the grandson of Genghis Khan.[41] The conquest of land that had been made by his grandfather was well known by people living in China. Throughout the region, even the mention of his name caused an upwelling of fear.

Before his death, Genghis Khan had controlled the biggest land empire in the world, including China, Mongolia, Persia, Northern India, Afghanistan, and most of Russia.

At the beginning of his rise to power, Genghis Khan coveted the wealth and the foods of China's great agricultural civilization. The success of the agricultural culture of China was epitomized by its great wealth. To Genghis Kahn, China was where the money was. That's where the silk was. That's where the food was. So he set about to conquer China.

To fend off continuous attacks by the Genghis Khan and his Mongolian warriors, China began building another section of the Great Wall of China.[42]

The conscripted laborers who built the wall and the Chinese soldiers who supervised them and guarded the wall required continuous massive amounts of rice and other grains to feed them.

The Great Wall was China's failed attempt to protect its rich agricultural land from nomadic and Mongolian invaders. Despite this monumental effort by the Chinese, Genghis Khan and his warriors made their way around, through, and over the wall into China.

Most people today have a negative image of Genghis Khan and the Mongols as barbarians. However, they were not just barbarians. Once they began to expand their territory into China, they became highly skilled at conducting business to expand their wealth and protecting the wealthy middlemen who sold goods along the Silk Roads that led to and from China. Genghis Khan's protection of middlemen also extended to business travelers from Western Europe.

Silk and other goods from China made their way westward to Europe along the Silk Roads; furs, amber, and other luxury good traveled east to China from Europe.

The rising demand for spices and sweets and Western Europe's desire to know more about this mysterious, faraway land grew so strong that it led to the Age of Exploration.[43]

Ships sailed out from every port in Europe in search of the spices that would bring their owners vast wealth. At that time, pepper, for example, was worth more than gold. So ships ventured around the world in search of the fabled Spice Islands. They also went in search of silk and other goods from the mystical land called China.

Their search for the Spice Islands and the wealth that a cargo of spices or silk could bring to the ship's owner also led to the accidental discovery of the Americas.

It would take almost 500 years and North America's growing focus on business and commerce—the import and exports of commodities—to lead the world to what it is today: a global network of transactions, including financial transactions and the two-way traffic of information and data.

The stability of the supply chain, over time, had become as invisible and seemingly as necessary to the global consumer as the oxygen we breathe and the blood that courses through our veins. Then, starting in 2020, the unexpected, world-wide impact of the COVID-19 pandemic disrupted the global supply chain. COVID-19 set in motion a series of events that would forever change the global supply chain.

The Modern Supply Chain

From the vantage point of an astronaut standing on the moon, the Earth looks like a small blue dot. As viewed from space, our tiny blue planet stands out as unique in the vast expanse of the universe.

If one were to zoom in for a closer look at the blue dot, they would first see a global network of lights that illuminate Earth 24 hours a day.

Zoom in closer and they would see white lines representing air traffic that transports more than one billion passengers and vast amounts of cargo each year.

Closer to ground level, a network of waterways and roads look to a casual observer like a maze with many twists and turns, with every choice leading to a destination or to a dead-end.

Objects floating on the surface of the oceans could be cargo ships, sailing vessels, or plastic trash. Pipelines and cables, unseen from above, crisscross the floor of the ocean.

These lights, lines, pipelines. cables, and waterways represent the multitude of routes that a global supply chain can take as it moves commodities, including grain, beef, luxury goods, oil, and natural gas, from place to place.

When there is a disruption in the supply chain, ripple effects are felt worldwide. This is because the modern-day supply chain is a complex, dynamic system. A small change—say, a reduction in the flow of oil and gas—can lead to a large-scale and unpredictable variation in the future state of the system.

The sensitivity of complex, dynamic systems was first described in 1961 by mathematician-turned-meteorologist Edward Lorenz, who coined the term *the butterfly effect*. Lorenz explained the widespread impact of a small variation in a dynamic weather system this way: "A butterfly flapping its wings in Brazil could set off a tornado in Texas."

To put this in the context of food, let's ask a simple question: Where does your food come from?

Is it a local? That is, is it grown somewhere within walking distance or a short drive from your home? Is it from a kitchen garden or backyard greenhouse where seasonal crops can be grown? Does it come from a larger plot of land that may include a fishpond, fruit trees, and a barn that provides shelter for pastured animals who provide eggs, milk, and meat for the table? A farmers market or local marketplace that features locally produced food?

Does some of your food come from far away?

Is it flown in from overseas or transported by cargo ship and then delivered to you by a network of railroads, delivery trucks, and vans? Is it sealed in a container wrapped in foil protected by polystyrene insulation, which is then surrounded by a cardboard box? Or is your food delivered on a wooden pallet to a grocery store, where the wooden pallet, cardboard box, polystyrene, and foil are all disposed of in a trash bin.

Prior to the arrival of the COVID-19 pandemic in America, most of us didn't pay much attention to where our food came from. We could simply stop by our favorite grocery store or order it for next-day delivery to our front door.

Then the proverbial"butterfly flapped its wings in 2020 and the COVID-19 pandemic impacted everything and everyone. Here's what happened next to disrupt America's food supply chain at home and worldwide over the next three years.

Lockdown: For the first year, until a vaccine slowly made its way into the public arena, everyone was advised to stay at home unless they need to shop for food or had an emergency and needed to seek medical help.

Shutdown: Most businesses were asked to send their employees home for their own health and safety if someone in their organization got the COVID-19 virus. If one person got it, there was a high risk that it would rapidly spread to the entire workforce. In one day, on March 18, 2020, Los Angeles County shut down 18 nonprofit organizations that prepared and delivered thousands of meals daily to the elderly and people with health issues. That was the day that we received a call from the director of that agency telling us that they had just shut the organizations down and asking if could we help.

Slowdown: There was panic shopping as people rushed to the grocery store to buy the store's supply of everything, needed or not, or just in case.

Closed: Restaurants were shut down due to the pandemic.

No Vacancy: Hotels, resorts, and ski towns shut down. Airlines reduced the number of flights per day. The polluted gray skies over major cities suddenly turned blue again.

Out of Stock: Most businesses that remained open during the pandemic posted "out of stock" signs reflecting the loss of goods from their suppliers or from business that had temporarily or permanently closed their doors.

Out of Business: Small businesses that lacked enough financial reserves to wait out the down time, loss of workers, and lost sales closed their doors for good.

Labor shortages impacted all of the above. People who were able to telecommute and work from home remained employed. Some moved to small rural towns or bought a van and worked from remote locations all across America. Those workers who lost their job, quit a bad job, went looking for a good job, or were underemployed were at risk of a loss of housing or, worse, eviction. For many of these people, their food purchasing power may have been reduced to food stamps.

Everyone in one way or another was caught up in the ripple effect of the COVID-19 pandemic, and taken all together, this added another level of stress to the supply chain.

Then there was a steady stream of bad news stories from the media and social media that reported on accidents that happened to cargo ships, cargo-carrying rail lines, and truck carrying cargo to every town in the US.

Take, for example, the *ONE Apus*, a 1,200-foot cargo ship delivering thousands of containers full of goods from China to Los Angeles. In remote waters 1,600 miles northwest of Hawaii, the container stack lashed to the ship's deck was struck by towering 30-foot waves. The stack collapsed, tossing more than 1,800 containers into the sea.

Remember the *Ever Given*, one of the largest container ships ever built, whose length was estimated to be as long as a skyscraper is tall? The *Ever Given* got stuck sideways in the Suez Canal for six days in March 2021. It backed up worldwide shipping on both ends of the canal. This supply chain disruption resulted in a loss of nearly $10 billion in trade a day.

For clothing retail shops, the delay and the ripple effect of months-long delays for unloading cargo at major ports like Long Beach, California, and elsewhere around the world meant that this year's fashion wear would now be "out of season" and would have to be sent to a discount clothing warehouse, with the upfront investment in the clothing written off as a loss. A cargo ship carrying 4,000 luxury cars sank. Cars worth $100,000 or more would soon provide underwater housing for fish and other sea creatures.

Then there was the theft of packages from porches, parked delivery vehicles, and rail cargo containers. Thieves in Los Angeles left the rail tracks beside idled trains littered with packages. Thieves stole bicycles, dismantled them, and sold those parts of the bike that were in high demand. They did the same with automobiles.

As the COVID-19 pandemic began to wind down, a convoy of truckers in Canada couldn't resist one last stand.

The blockage of the supply chain across a major bridge crossing between the US and Canada by truckers protesting against vaccine rules created weeks of gridlock on both sides of the border.

The *New York Times* reported that the truckers' traffic-blocking tactics had spread to other Canadian cities, including Toronto, Quebec City, and Calgary. For nearly a week the truck blockade jammed the Ambassador Bridge, which links Windsor, Ontario, to Detroit, Michigan, stopping all traffic. That crossing normally carries $300 million worth of goods a day.

According to Canada's finance minister, the economic impact to the supply chain from trucker convoy protests at border crossings across the country impacted more than $500 million in commerce each day.[44]

Post-COVID-19 Supply Chain

Today the global supply chain is not simply disrupted; it is broken. Absolute control of a resource and its distribution is no longer the key to wealth and power—innovation is, according to Andy Kessler, an opinion columnist for the *Wall Street Journal*.[45]

Kessler uses the terms *horizonal* and *vertical* to differentiate between the wealth and global power of innovative horizonal companies such as Google, Apple, and Amazon, who rely on layers of innovation from the bottom to the top as the key to their success, and vertical organizations such as Putin's empire, which he predicts is doomed to fail. "You don't invade countries anymore because after the smoke clears, you have to fix their plumbing and heating and cell service. Instead, you hire them."

The modern supply chain is broken, precisely because of its top-down control of resources and their distribution. We were warned about this danger by US president Dwight D. Eisenhower in a speech he made in 1961. "Beware of the military-industrial complex," Eisenhower warned the American public as he was retiring as head of the US government and as supreme Allied commander of the European Theater of Operations during World War II. What Eisenhower had been seeking was peace and prosperity for all. Some historians would say this warning was his greatest contribution to world peace and the common good.

He was talking about the revolving door between military leaders and a global network of major defense contractors. Upon retirement, military leaders might be offered lucrative salaries to join a major defense contractor. Their job would be to secure a continuous flow of government contracts that could lock in a country's commitment to purchase arms, equipment, and fuel from a single contractor for many years.

Fast-forward to the start of the 1980s, when a shortage of oil and gas from OPEC resulted in a gas shortage for the Western world. Worldwide, the news media carried images of long lines of cars and people holding gas cans waiting for a turn at the gas pump.

In 2002, the Iraq War brought US military troops to the Middle East to protect Western interests in Iraq's oil fields. This military intervention highlighted the growing dependence of the West on foreign oil and gas. However, the irony of sending US troops to protect their oil fields was perhaps best illustrated by a now famous war protest sign that was broadcast worldwide: "Why is OUR oil underneath THEIR sand?"

It would take another twenty years for the Western world to become united in its commitment to break its own addiction to fossil fuels. The reason for this butterfly effect was unexpected, and it would set in motion actions that would begin the uncoupling of oil and gas as the world's primary energy source.

It began with Putin's war on Ukraine, which pitted Russia's military might against its neighbor. As the first shots were fired, the Western world quickly learned two important things.

The first was that Ukrainian countryside, which has perhaps the best soil for growing crops in the world, also serves as a vital transportation corridor for Russian pipelines. These pipelines connect Russia's oil and gas fields to the fossil fuel-dependent countries that make up the European Union. Germany relies on Russia for two-thirds of its gas supply.

The second thing that became public knowledge was the fact that 60 percent of the Russian economy is based on fossil fuels.[46] This, in essence is its Achilles' heel. Russia depends on the sale and transportation of fossil fuels for its own economic stability. Sixty-five percent of Russia's landmass is covered in melting permafrost. Climate change and rising temperatures are having a disastrous effect on rail lines, roads, and fossil fuel infrastructure.[47]

And we all learned one thing more, which turned out to be the key reason why the Western world was able to mobilize so quickly against their own financial interests and their own preference for a diplomatic solution: the resiliency and capacity for heroic actions of the people of Ukraine.

When offered a chance to escape the conflict and lead his people from a safe location in another country, Ukrainian president Volodymyr Zelensky told the US and the world: "I need ammunition, not a ride."

"Their resistance against fearsome odds," wrote the editorial board of the *Wall Street Journal*, "is an inspiration and has awakened the world to the menace of the Kremlin autocrat."

A fearless defense of our family, our country, and our freedom lies at the core of all that makes us human. The fearless actions of the Ukrainian people inspired us to become bold and fearless.

Today, the lives and livelihoods of people around the world are intertwined. We have come to expect that what we want or need will come from close to home or far away. Either way, we depend on the timely transport of commodities from around the globe.

A quick look around our home, for example, reveals that most of our furniture, appliances, electronics, clothing, and food comes from somewhere else around the world.

Yet these goods, brought to us by a well-functioning supply chain, are only the tip of the iceberg.

What lies beneath the surface is a worldwide flow of information, a global network of continuously updated financial transactions. The round-the-clock flow of these electronic transactions via satellite, cable, and the internet function somewhat like the blood that flows to and from the human heart through arteries, veins, and capillaries to the farthest reaches of the human body and back again. If the heart stops beating, the blood stops flowing.

Today, when the flow of money needed to keep commodities moving is blocked—in the case of Putin's war, by economic sanctions mobilized by a coalition of world leaders against Russia—the result is the economic equivalent of a heart attack to the country (or countries) most affected by this action.

For example, a freeze in financial assets, a denial of the right to land an airplane at an international airport or unload cargo at a shipping hub, or even a steady decline in demand for gas and oil over time, say some economists, could reduce a global power such as Russia to a dependent economy.

Russia's invasion of its neighbor Ukraine, in short, became "the shot heard round the world." Overnight, everything changed.

For the first time since World War II the Western world was willing to suffer supply chain disruptions that would impact their own comfortable lifestyle along with the risk of inflation as they unified around a common goal.

"The world is now so wired, superempowered individuals, companies and social activist groups can pile on their own sanctions and boycotts, *without any government orders*," wrote economist Thomas L. Friedman in an opinion column. "Rarely, if ever, has a country this big and powerful been politically cancelled and economically crippled so fast."[48]

At times of great change, it often takes a major breakdown to create a breakthrough.

Take concrete, for example. A sidewalk made of concrete can be broken down by tiny cracks that emerge over time. Tiny grass seeds that land on the concrete will send their roots down through the cracks and into the soil beneath. This is also true of asphalt. A newly paved street that has a crack will begin to sprout a plant, a tiny flower. It can be a harbinger of things to come.

The same is true of the worldly ambitions of a global superpower. Beware of the military-industrial complex, President Eisenhower warned.

So, at a time when Russia was exercising its military might in Ukraine and China was winding down its New Year's celebrations, 2022 became a tipping point that forged a new determination for America and its allies to move beyond their dependence on fossil fuels. The path they had embarked on together, they believed, would lead to a safer world, with more economic stability for everyone.

Three trends over time have been converging on this moment in time to disrupt our dependence on food, oil and gas, and luxury goods from around the world. The perfect storm that has been brewing over many years is the result of a convergence of three major factors:

1. Energy from oil and gas, including natural gas
2. Energy from solar and other renewable energy and energy efficiency.
3. The COVID-19 pandemic and globe-traveling viruses

The future supply chain for food, many experts now agree, will be seasonal, bioregional, hyperlocal, and horizonal. Every horizonal layer is made up of many food innovators who contribute to the supply chain from the farm to the table.

The community, which sits on top, will prosper because of the economic stability of the layers and the fact that the revenue will trickle up to the top, as sales tax from purchases made in the community, property tax, and an improvement in the health and well-being of residents from a shift to fresh, healthy, locally sourced produce and products.

Innovations and timely solutions can tip the economy away from a dependence on fossil fuels toward sustainability, community resiliency, solar energy, renewable resources, and energy efficiency. The innovations include:

- A 15-minute city is a community identified within a larger urban area that offers easy walking or bicycling access to food, transportation, healthcare, kindergarten through college education, and government services within a 15-minute walk from your front door.[49]

- Vertical gardens, greenhouses, and indoor gardening innovations provide ongoing protection from climate impacts and high levels of ultraviolet radiation.[50]
- New nutrition makes the shift from wheat, rice, corn, and barley to the meals that include 50 percent fiber-rich, nutrient-dense foods.[51]
- Watch the documentary *Milked* to learn about perfect foods and discover what makes Impossible Burgers possible.[52]
- In 2022 New York City mayor Eric Adams launched a new healthcare-based initiative called the Plant-Based Lifestyle Medicine Program.[53]
- *The Nine Nations of North America* by Joel Garreau describes nine bioregions and underscores why hyper-local and regionally sourced foods represents the future of the food security.[54]
- Victory gardens, kitchen gardens, indoor gardens, and community gardens can supply local food. Got an abandoned freeway in your city? Turn it into an arial garden for local food producers. Need to clean up a river that is linked to the ocean? Fill it up with a billion oysters. They can clean up polluted waterways and serve as a future food source.[55]
- Nutrition education courses can help you improve your family's health. Visit a local food hub or farmers market. Learn the names of the local farmers who grow the food you buy.[56]

- Do you know someone on food stamps? Did you know that food stamps can be used to purchase fresh produce at a farmer's market? A First Food Responder or Zipper can be handed these ingredients and turn them into a week's worth of meals.[57]
- Elementary students in any community can become Green Leaders when they answer 21 questions at sustainability2020.org. The online questionnaire helps them conduct an energy audit in their own home. The collected data can then be used by the sustainability director in any forward-thinking community to make bulk purchases of appliances, lighting, and roof insulation and offer those items for free or with a zero-interest or low-interest loan.[58]

Chapter 5

Feeding and Healing the Heart of Community One Meal at a Time

W hen a person goes into a home improvement center to purchase a power tool such as an electric lawn mower, the first question they might ask the clerk is "How does it work?" In response, the clerk may describe its key features and then hand the customer an instruction guide and tell them, "All you need to know on how to keep it running smoothly is in this little booklet."

Whether you are buying a power tool for your home, a smartphone, a house cleaning robot, or a new automobile, each of these come with instructions on how to use it and how to keep it finely tuned.

By contrast, what happens when a baby is born? The first thing new parents are told is "It's a boy" or "It's a girl." There is no owner's manual for how to maintain or fine-tune the human body. In terms of food, what does it take to raise a strong, healthy baby so that it can grow up to reach its full potential as a human being?

Sometimes, the most important things a person needs to learn during their lifetime to fully express their potential is discovered at the end of a lifetime, and begins with the phrase: "I never knew that…"

I never knew that eating certain foods could have helped me prevent this disease.

I never knew that fiber-rich, nutrient-dense fruits and vegetables could help me treat my high blood pressure, my obesity, my type 2 diabetes, heart disease, stress, anxiety, depression, dementia…[59]

I never knew that my heart is a muscle and that even a small amount of aerobic exercise, as little as five minutes a day, would have helped me keep it strong.

I never knew that boosting soft, green vegetables like spinach, collard greens, or kale to 50 percent or more at meal-time might have helped prevent my colorectal cancer.[60]

In truth, there has never been an owner's manual for the human body until now. Now, at last, we know how to design each meal and that doing even a small amount of aerobic exercise every day can help us achieve and maintain a high level of health, including mental health, mental well-being, and happiness.

Did you know that your gut is called the second brain?[61] That's where 50 trillion bacteria live. When you feed them their favorite greens, they repay you by producing good chemicals that keep you happy. The path to happiness, scientists tell us, is through your gut.

Where has this newly discovered owner's manual been hidden until now? For the answer, look within.

Maintaining your good health and mental health starts from the inside out. It begins with daily habit formation. It's what you eat and your ability to start and maintain a healthy exercise routine over time. Both the fresh, healthy food you eat and a daily exercise routine enable you to say hello to good health, high energy levels, and mental clarity and say goodbye to brain fog.

The path to a plant-based lifestyle medicine began in 1899, just before the start of the 20th century, in Lake Placid, New York, at a series of conferences on home economics.

Little was known about the many health benefits of fiber-rich, nutrient-dense foods, perhaps because it was part of everyday life. People were not obese or dying of heart attacks, cancer, type 2 diabetes, or similar diseases.

At that time, most of America was rural, and almost all of the food that was prepared and served at every meal was fiber-rich, nutrient-dense, and home-cooked. The vegetables, fruits, good oils, and protein were home-grown or purchased from local farmers.

In 1899, no one could prove scientifically that an active lifestyle would both strengthen your heart and stimulate the growth of new brain cells. However, the very lifestyle of a farm family brought them these benefits because each day came with a list of daily chores. Parents and kids walked or ran to and from the field to the barn, or to and from town. Harvest time included twisting, turning, and lifting, activities that are seen today in workout routines at a local gym.

It would take many more years of research before the discoveries about the many benefits of eating fresh, healthy food and a daily exercise routine would be reported as "breaking news" in the medical journals.

Today, what is revealed by researchers in the medical world can take 35 years or longer to become widespread public knowledge.

For example, very few people know that when you grow new brain cells through aerobic activity, you can grow smarter.[62] This happens because these new brain cells are waiting for you to set up a new habit that will give them something to do, such as learn a new skill or learn how to prepare and eat better food.

At the series of groundbreaking science-based conferences in Lake Placid, where a group of female scholars discussed their latest research on the nutritional value of food with the audience, they had focused on how it could be applied at the community level and to household work. They also described the best practices for childcare.

Over time the science-based research discussed at these conferences formed the basis of home economics classes that would be part of a required curriculum for students, especially young teenage girls in schools across America.

Remember the home economics class that your grandparents, parents, and perhaps even you had to take in middle school or high school? In those classes you may have learned how to make a meal for dinner and then eat it. Perhaps you learned to make lasagna, meatloaf, or tuna noodle casserole. You might have even learned how to make a delicious tiramisu or chocolate mousse.

Perhaps you learned food preparation, followed by a class where you learned how to sew your own clothing, including an apron.

After World War II and through the 1970s, the focus on home economics began to shift toward the burden of household work and the redefinition of the housewife as an unpaid "home engineer." It was no longer listed as a required class.

The declining interest in home economics was followed by growing awareness of women's economic self-reliance as they entered the American workforce in ever greater numbers.

Classes in home economics were dropped from many course catalogs in middle and high school and at the university or community college level.

These classes were not just dropped because of a lack of student interest. The rise of a global supply chain was also driving this downward trend away from learning how to prepare a home-cooked meal or make your own clothing.

Highly processed foods that were harvested, processed, and turned into manufactured food that had a long shelf life, or frozen foods that one could just "heat and eat," began to replace fresh, local, fiber-rich home-cooked foods.

There was a rise in fast-food drive-throughs, diners, convenience stores, and shopping malls with food courts. There was a surplus of food from around the world that could be purchased year-round regardless of the season.

By 1986, the University of Iowa's reason for eliminating its home economics classes was primarily due to a major shift in local farm practices. Iowa's rich farmland and dark soil, which could grow almost any kind of food, was being converted to monocrop farming. The single crop that was replacing a diversity of crops was corn. With a growing interest in corn for biofuels and animal feed, local farmers quickly realized that a much higher profit could be made from growing corn.

In the early 1990s, 92 percent of the food that showed up on the dinner table or in a local restaurant in Iowa had been shipped into the state by railcar or cargo truck from elsewhere to feed residents.

At high schools and colleges across the US, few people were interested in the subject of home economics. What caught their interest were coupons that offered discounts or "buy-one-get-one-free" specials on new products on grocery store shelves.

It would take another 20 years for home economics classes to resurface in the classroom. And when they did, the classes would be rebranded as "human ecology."[63]

Students were becoming more interested in science, technology, engineering, and medicine. For those who had an interest in food, human ecology classes offered science-based research and student collaboration with other departments.

At college level, these science-based classes included collaboration with students who were earning degrees in engineering, life, environmental sciences, or medicine.

Students in human ecology could major in family ecology, textiles, fashion design, clothing, community nutrition, or child and youth studies.

Today courses have added a focus on food as medicine, now referred to plant-based lifestyle medicine because it includes a focus on both food and exercise—that is, the whole body.[64] Courses are also offered that include research on work-life balance, the ecology of the workplace, and on how to manage problems you might face in your own home. Classes in nutritional education and family relations are also popular with students.

In the pandemic era, where disruptions in the global supply chain for grains due to weather events or war are ever present, there is growing interest in learning how to prepare an anti-inflammatory meal from local produce and products for yourself or an individual with a health problem, or perhaps a child from a low-income family to help them eat better food.

Classes that focus on local agriculture and family farms may now include a study of regenerative farming practices, farmers markets, and a new trend called food pharmacy, which is a farm-to-table approach to locally source healthy foods and, perhaps most importantly, community food security.[65]

You can give a person food, or you can teach them how to prepare their own fresh, healthy meals.

Today, scientific research and successful clinical trials are reminding a new generation of home cooks of the long-forgotten truth that healthy food can be more than medicine; it can reduce mental fog, boost energy levels, and improve mental health.

Healthy food, when incorporated into a daily meal plan, can also help cut hospital admissions by 50 percent and reduce healthcare costs by 16 percent, especially for those individuals with type 2 diabetes and low-income mothers. Patients who receive medically tailored meals experience 50 percent fewer hospitalizations and 72 percent fewer skilled nursing facility admissions.[66]

The good news we're learning is this: The owner's manual for fine-tuning the human body to keep it in good working condition is being written right now, in our own lifetime.

Happily, you don't have to have gone to college to learn how to apply this to your own life. Anyone with computer or smartphone access can now take self-paced classes that can be custom-fit to your specific interests.

You can gain practical experience preparing meals for others in a commercial training kitchen. You can learn how to plan, prep, and serve a delicious, homemade, healthy meal in less than 20 minutes that can improve your own health and the health of your family.

Right now is a great time to be someone who loves to cook, whether you are rich or poor, have a college degree or none, or were born here or somewhere else. The home cook is on the front lines of community food security.

"When I turned 40," Sonya told me over the phone, "my husband thought I was no longer beautiful, so he threw me out on the porch like an old couch. "As Sonya slowly and painfully recounted this traumatic moment in her life to me, I felt my eyes began to fill with tears.

The reason for my call was to learn more about her cooking skills and to get a better understanding of what had driven her to follow this new career path.

Sonya talked about the three months she and her young son were homeless. They had spent three months living in her car until a social worker had finally been able to help her move into a permanent home in a nearby affordable housing complex.

Sonya was lucky. Her new home also included a kitchen.

As her conversations became more self-reflective, she shared a little more of her journey to what she now called "her dream job."

An immigrant from Brazil, with a warm, friendly smile, Sonya had been quickly offered an entry-level job with a catering service in Hollywood whose clientele were celebrities and politicians. In time, she would fall in love, marry, work while pregnant, and then return to her job at the catering company after the birth of her son.

Looking back on those hard times, she added, "No one ever valued me for my real talent, which is my cooking skills."

Sonya and I had met because a simple two-line ad had caught her eye. It began: "If you love to cook and have a home kitchen…"

Sonya took two months to go through the basic steps that would lead to licensing and certification. The training program, which included mentorship, began with an online food handler's course, followed by a kitchen safety manager training program, and a deep dive into food safety, including the safe storage and delivery of food.

Although Sonya did not consider herself tech-savvy, she quickly learned how to take online courses and was successful at passing the proctored final exam.

The online training was followed by hands-on menu planning and compiling a list of ingredients for each meal, which included the nutritional values of food and food safety considerations. Then the program shifted to hands-on experience in purchasing and preparing ingredients for a meal, temperature control, and safe delivery to a designated location.

If this sounds impossible, it's not. It's what happens in every kitchen around the world several times a day. It's not rocket science. People prepare food for themselves; they prepare and serve meals for their family and for their friends. And, at the end of the meal, we get up from the table and offer our complements to the chef or whoever prepared the meal.

Sometimes, among friends, the meal is a potluck, and everyone brings their favorite homemade dish to share. Potlucks are a bit like a tasting fair, where we get a chance to experience a variety of cuisines and cultures as we move from one serving dish to the next.

Handmade food prepared on a camping trip in a pot or pan perched on top of a tiny cookstove or at a campground on a grill may include the scent of pine trees, wild grass at the edge of a lake, wildflowers, or smoke from a fire. You may taste the essence of pine.

The good news about preparing delicious meals for yourself, your family, and your friends is that anyone can do this, any time of the day or night. It's legal everywhere in the world.

However, when you take your love of cooking and expand it to the next level to help feed hungry people in your community, you must be trained, licensed, and certified.

As a First Food Responder, for example, you will be trained in safe food storage, healthy meal preparation and the safe delivery of food to others in a three-month program that pays you for your service to others.

In the process you are turning your love of cooking into a micro-enterprise business.

Whether you are legally able to prepare meals from your own home kitchen or you are required to prepare meals at a nearby commercial kitchen, you will be able to make enough money to pay your bills from a job that is linked to your passion and skills.

You will then be able to lead by example, as you transfer your new knowledge of the importance of fiber-rich foods and nutrition to other people in your community.

They will notice your energy level, your positive attitude, and your growing sense of confidence. You are helping make the world a better place, one meal at a time.

"When you learn something, share something," poet laureate Maya Angelou said. So, if you love to cook and have a home kitchen, here are some pathways that can lead you to a new career and enough money to pay your bills.

A Final Note

According to the *International Encyclopedia of the Social and Behavioral Sciences*,

The evolutionary theory frame [of human ecology] covers applications of natural selection to the ecological behavior of individuals and groups or populations, including the demographic and social epidemiology of pathogenic disease. The environmental theory frame covers the mixing of biological and social theory and fact for application to nature-society interactions. It covers applications of natural selection to the ecological behavior of individuals and groups or populations, including the demographic and social epidemiology of pathogenic disease. The analogic-symbolic theory frame covers applications of ecological metaphor to questions of social science. The interactive theory frame covers applications to develop ecology as a world view for deriving value judgments intended to promote political, cultural, or individual change in human priorities.[67]

Why is this important? Ask a scientist or take a course human ecology and learn how #changethroughfood can happen in your community.

Chapter 6

The Big Quit

Cities and Businesses Must Reinvent Themselves

I n early 2020, global news headlines began to warn the public about a deadly coronavirus spreading through airports and flights around the world. The virus would begin to show up as flu-like symptoms in an unsuspecting air traveler. As the symptoms got worse, the now highly contagious traveler would be sent to a local hospital, where they would be placed in quarantine. There would be an attempt to reach out to other passengers who had been traveling on the same airplane, and any other people they may have come in contact with prior to their arrival at the hospital. This happened to America's patient number 1.

Multiply that scenario by millions of people worldwide who had been exposed to COVID-19 by a stranger or someone they knew, and you have an idea of the challenges that lay ahead for the world as it spiraled downward into lockdown.[68]

By March 2020, millions of working parents—who had made up a key part of the labor force for restaurants, hotels, and the retail industry—began to receive termination notices from their employers. They were told that the business where they had been employed was closing its doors due to a lack of customers. They might be called back to work if the business was able reopen its doors again sometime in the uncertain future.

By mid-March, people traveling by car, say, from California through Arizona and Utah to Colorado along the interstate highways, would have quickly noticed signs of a looming shutdown of business at every stop they made along the way.

Perhaps they had also been warned by family members or friends to avoid using the public restroom at gas stations along the way. The restrooms had become hotspots for the deadly virus. All it would take was for one coronavirus infected person to cough or sneeze, and the next 100 people who entered the poorly ventilated room after them would most likely become infected as well.

Public fear was on the rise.

Cross-country travelers would also be worried that if one of the people in the car became sick before they reached their destination, everyone riding in the car might be placed in quarantine in an unfamiliar town along the way.

Worse, a small-town clinic might not have the type of medical equipment needed to treat a traveler who had fallen sick with COVID-19.

Interstate travelers returning home from a holiday during the early days of the pandemic would also be taking a gamble that gas stations and overnight lodging would still be open to welcome them.

Overhead highway signs along the route that warned travelers of road conditions ahead now included a bold warning: AVOID COVID-19.

To the frontline workers who managed the cash registers at convenience stores or front desks at motels, every traveler who showed up in their small town was a potential carrier of the deadly virus.

When the eastbound travelers were finally greeted by a WELCOME TO COLORADO billboard, they also saw a sign that reminded that Colorado was SKI COUNTRY USA.

Colorado's sunny skies and well-groomed ski slopes are world famous. For more than 50 years, the ski trails of celebrities and locals have crisscrossed one another on the downhill runs.

So imagine the surprise of a traveler as their car sped past Beaver Creek, Vail, and Copper Mountain. These world-famous ski towns that were normally overbooked and overcrowded now had the look of ghost towns.

The lights were out at hotels and condos and restaurants. Mile after mile, the scene that unfolded was the same. It was as if time stood still and all the people had disappeared.

The date was March 16. Lockdown had begun. They would be able to arrive home before dark, unpack the car, and assess what would be needed to plan for the long and uncertain future that lay ahead.

Lockdown rules around the world required that people stay at home. People were advised to only leave their home for essential errands like the purchase of food and medicine or a medical appointment.

Everyone now wore a mask. They avoided eye contact with strangers. They were uncertain whether they should shake someone's hand or bump elbows as a greeting. They were suspicious of what lingered on the surface of a tabletop, suspicious of a possible health risk from a simple exhale of breath from someone walking in front of them. Even when they purchased their groceries from the store, they would wipe down each item before putting it away in their home.

How long did the coronavirus linger in the air? Even visiting family members represented a health risk. Who had they been in contact with before they arrive at the front door?

When the summer of 2020 arrived, restrictions eased briefly, only to be tightened up again in a few short months. While some of the people who had been among the first to lose their jobs were still waiting for unemployment payments to begin, a second wave of workers began to decide that now was the perfect time to resign, effective immediately.

Those who were fully employed or underemployed at the time who decided to give up, pack up, and head out "anywhere but here" were among the first to launch the Big Quit movement. Some people planned to be gone for only a year. It would be a gap year. A sabbatical. A reboot. They would rent out their home, go on a trip, and return at some later date. Or they would sell their house, buy a van, and re-create a new life at a mobile home in the great outdoors.

Those who formally resigned from the workforce, or who simply called in sick to work and never returned to the office, were soon followed by millions of other Americans.

The reasons that they gave were as varied as their life circumstances. They may have been trapped in lockdown with an angry or abusive partner. They may have simply had enough of a sedentary lifestyle or of urban or suburban living. Living a "normal life" may have no longer seemed possible. Maybe they realized how burnt out they were from their job.

Among the outspoken advocates of the Big Quit were the nearly three million working moms who had been unable to find adequate, safe, or affordable childcare.[69] Or they were the working moms who found themselves balancing a toddler on their knee or breastfeeding an infant during a Zoom meeting. The search for support services, including childcare, put a strain on every working parent.

Parents who finally said "I quit" had tried to balance work and life with their children at home and failed. So, they looked for another way to stabilize their family life.

Announcing "I quit" offered a way for those who joined the movement to say to themselves and to anyone who would listen that it was time to reinvent themselves and find the perfect job that matched their talents and passion. For some, it also meant that it was time for them to turn their back on the past and head in a new direction and possibly start their own business.

This second wave of COVID was labeled by the news media as the Big Quit, and it marked a convergence of events during the lockdown period that would become a tipping point from which there would be no return.[70] No going back to business as usual.

The convergence of events during lockdown that turned into a perfect storm included an unrelenting stream of bad news about the deadly impact of the coronavirus that showed up 24/7 in their social media feeds and all the news channels.

The troubling news stories and images aggregated from around the world were counterbalanced by business success stories that highlighted breaking news for rapidly evolving AI technology. The dream of a technology-driven future was beginning to erode the dream of job security for a future workforce.

Adding to the stress were trending news stories from around the world that offered viewers a video loop of an extreme climate events that—at that very moment—were destroying the homes, lives, and livelihoods of people just like them. The message: It could happen, at any moment, to any of us.

And perhaps the last straw was the stark news from healthcare experts that the deadly coronavirus that had killed millions worldwide would soon begin mutating into new strains.

In year 2 of the COVID-19 pandemic, four new viruses had been identified.

The appearance of Delta, Omicron, BA1, BA2, and other virus variants sent another shock wave around the globe.

It wasn't just personal stress and anxiety caused by two years of lockdown that led to the Big Quit. It wasn't even the hotly debated mask mandates that lit the fire in the belly of millions of Americans who decided to get up and walk away from the workplace.

The spark that lit the fire that motivated the Big Quit movement was the sudden realization that their own personal health and the health of their family had to become their number one priority. In a world that seemed to be falling apart, they had to find a way to stay both healthy and sane.

The important questions people were asking were quite revealing: Why do I need a nine-to-five job? Why do I need a steady paycheck? Isn't it about time that I took a few risks in life, especially now, when my own health or life might be suddenly taken away from me by the coronavirus?

Over time, this small, steady stream of Americans leaving the American workforce became a tsunami.

Risk-taking was on the rise. Everyone had a story to tell about what had pushed them to the brink.

Those who said goodbye to a corporate job to take a gap year to travel may have left by telling themselves or others that they would only be gone for a year. They would be taking a break. They needed time off for rest and recovery. They would return to the office sometime next year.

There were also the millions of burned-out, worn-out, totally exhausted healthcare workers who turned away and walked away from their high-risk job.

The patient loads these overworked health workers had been required to handle, even when they themselves might be sick with COVID-10, were the result of a labor shortage. These healthcare workers were also maxed out from the continuous trauma of dealing with fearful, sick, and dying people and having to tell worried family members that someone they loved had just died. And so, they finally said, "I quit."[71]

People walked away from good jobs and bad jobs, from low-paying jobs where wages had been stagnant for years, and from other jobs because of the uncertainty of whether the business owner—struggling to meet the monthly payroll—would be able to keep their doors open for customers.

The Great Renegotiation

This mass resignation of America's workforce shook the very foundation of corporate America and Main Street businesses across the country.[72] What would lure skilled workers back to the office?

If telecommuting to work from home wasn't enough of a perk, if an economic stimulus check to help them pay their bills while out of work was no longer an option, if the return to health of a sick family member wasn't enough to bring them back to the office or the workforce after the lockdown was over, what would bring them back? The employee now had the upper hand.

Free childcare? Free transportation to and from work? Free lunches? Stock options? Employee ownership? An apartment with a view in a rent-controlled building in the center of town that a labor-short corporation had just purchased?

It was time for business-minded employers to change their strategy, not turn back the clock to pre-pandemic times. Changing their strategy meant reinventing the workplace, the economy, and the future of work to benefit the employees as well as their business.

There was a great advantage to many employers using remote workforces, too. They would now have a much lower overhead because they did not need as much office space with all the virtual workers—or maybe no office space at all.

Everything that had once seemed to work perfectly now had to be reimagined.

Downtown office buildings were at risk of losing long-term corporate tenants when their leases expired.[73] Who would rent the empty office space? Who would pay the city sales tax or property tax? Who would want to ride alone in an elevator to the top floor of an empty office building, even though the offices on the top floor offered the best view of the city?

City and county government leaders across the US would have to reimagine their local economy by looking at new sources of revenue that would help counter the lost sales tax, property tax, and other line items in their operating budget derived from commuters.

Reimagining local housing security, food security, and job security that meets the needs of today's multigenerational workforce will help create local economic security and sustainability.[74]

The Coming Great Retirement

A generational hand-off is occurring right now in the American workplace. As baby boomers retire, generation X accounts for 51 percent of leadership roles.[75] By 2025, millennials will make up more than 75 percent of the global workforce.[76]

With an aging population and hungry humans in mind, who among today's traditionalists, boomers, generation Xers, and millennials would jump at the chance to be paid to prepare and deliver fresh, delicious home-cooked meals to the elderly, people with health issues, or hungry children? Who among those swept up in the coming Great Retirement will need additional income to help them pay their bills as a First Food Responder?

Learn more about how to get involved as a cook or contributor in chapter 8.

Chapter 7

What Is the Fix?

Starting a New Career

With a passion for innovation and social good that sparks breakthrough thinking about what works and what is possible, I set out to make a difference in the world of the home cook.

To be honest, I'm not a good cook—not by a long shot—but what I had going for me when I first decided to enter the unfamiliar territory of a home kitchen was a sense of immense purpose.

And one thing more. In 2019, I had published a little book on food called *23Ingredients Menu Planner*. The book addresses both food security, with healthy food choices, and food poverty, with a $5/day cost. It captured the imagination of several people who would eventually become collaborators in creating a vision to harness the untapped power of home cooks.

I met these three collaborators that spring at an event called Earth's Call at the Aspen Institute. My expertise at the time was not home cooking. It was women's leadership.

What inspired the innovators I met in Aspen was the simple concept behind my new book. I had designed it as a universal meal planner. It was a single recipe that could be adapted to match seasonal, local, and available produce and farm products anywhere in the world.

The mission of the little book was to help people eat better food. It focused on 50 years' worth of science-based research on how to achieve optimum health through a plant-based, nutrient-dense, fiber-rich meal. It built a bridge between vegan, vegetarian, paleo, and ketogenic lifestyles and brings out the best from each.

To my surprise and delight, when the idea of collaboration on a grant was presented to Daniel Taylor, the visionary president of Future Generations University, by one of his students, Rosalie Pearl Lynch, Taylor was immediately interested.

Taylor had formerly served as chair of the Department of Nutrition at John Hopkins medical school. However, in 1990, with funding provided by UNICEF, he launched Future Generations University. The university was soon offering an online master's degree in applied community change in 40 countries around the world. The concept of #ChangeThrough-Food appealed to him.

Environmentalist Bill McKibben wrote that Taylor's mantra is "Forget big plans. Development is not a product, not a target, not some happy future state…it's a process, measured not in budgets but in how we invest our human energy."[77] McKibben was inspired by Taylor's work.

In turn, Taylor became inspired by a future vision of home cooks as First Food Responders who could create community change from their own licensed and certified home kitchen or a commercial kitchen. The program as envisioned would engage a hyperlocal network of home cooks who could help ensure food security and resiliency in their own community—wherever they lived in the world.

Taylor was also interested in offering the program as a master's degree option for his university students. It appealed to him because the program would include online and applied learning as well as project-based research and personal leadership development.

Interested students from around the world who enrolled as master's students could be trained to set up a pilot program in their own community.

They would learn about successful public outreach techniques. They would invite the participation of local home cooks who had already learned the art and skill of making a good meal. The students would then mentor the home cooks through the training and food safety protocol courses that concluded with licensing and certification.

In the process, they would also be able to engage with local food-hub organizations and farmers, receive on-the-job nutrition education, and be able to identify and measure the best practices for implementation of the program in their community. As part of their future career, the students would monitor improvements in the physical health and mental well-being of program participants and the vulnerable populations they served, and then submit a final report to complete their degree. It was a win-win for all.

A second collaborator was Matthew Scherr. At the time, Scherr was a county commissioner for Eagle County, Colorado. The county includes two world-famous ski areas: Vail and Beaver Creek. Scherr also served on the Vail Valley Partnership Economic Development Leadership Council.

The population they serve includes active sports tourists and people who call Eagle County home. Of the 55,000 county residents, many of whom work in the hospitality industry, one-third are Latino. There is a higher population of young Latinos in the local schools than other cultures. Many don't speak English. The county is considered a food desert. Its residents have limited access to urgent care clinics and hospital services.

Inspired by a vision of uplifting the lives of people in poverty through food, Scherr agreed that a pilot program designed to benefit human health across all ages and racial, socioeconomic, religious, gender, cognitive, cultural, and political spectrums would be welcome in his county.

The emerging vision of First Food Responders took another step forward toward becoming a reality.

The third person to think together with us on how to make this happen was Doug Hofmeister, a retired executive from IBM. As founder and vice chairman of MarketSquare, Hofmeister was involved in a new startup. His focus was on how to use blockchain technology to connect local farmers to nearby communities—in this case, to future licensed home cooks. Local farmers would be able provide home cooks with fresh, local, seasonal foods at fair market price for use in preparing delicious home-cooked food for the food insecure in their community.

All three of these talented leaders understood the concept of exponential growth. If you get a program right in one location, it is possible to scale it to meet the same or similar needs in other communities.

Here's one example of how a successful First Food Responders program might scale to a low-income community in any rural or urban area—Poughkeepsie, New York; Hailey, Idaho; or Hemet, California, for example.

Add in any of the 10 major climate impact disaster areas across the US that are continuously hit by tornados, hurricanes, wildfires, or flooding year after year. These events demand a continuous infusion of disaster-related funding for essential services like meal service.

Worldwide, similar events unfold 24/7 and are reported through the news media and social media. Less known, however, are the hidden pockets of hunger that remain invisible to all but a few humanitarian agencies. Take the African country of Uganda, for example, and a community of 28,000 grandmothers.

Uganda is the home country of Rehmah Kasule, a young leader I met in 2013, when I served as her mentor on a leadership program funded by UN-Habitat.

Every Monday morning for 18 months, I spent an hour with Rehmah via Skype. Her goal was to lift 200 young women out of the slums of Kampala, Uganda, by providing them with micro entrepreneurship skills, mentorship, and leadership training, and she was successful.

In October 2014, Rehmah became *Fortune* magazine's number one Social Impact Entrepreneur in the world at the *Fortune*/Goldman Sachs "Most Powerful Women in the World" summit. The following year, her slum women project (SWEEP), which had also received funding from the MacArthur Foundation, won acclaim as the "Most Sustainable Program" across the entire continent of Africa.

Mentorship goes both ways. Over the years, Rehmah and I have remained in contact. We have continued to learn from each other.

In Spring 2022, Rehmah and I connected via Zoom to discuss how our First Food Responder program could be launched in several communities in Africa.

One of particular interest to Rehmah was a village of 28,000 grandmothers who had been left in charge of their grandchildren after their parents died of AIDS. On our phone call, Rehmah and I discussed the possibility of setting up a train-the-trainers program to teach a group of grandmothers who were skilled home cooks how to become First Food Responders.

Not all people are great cooks. However, interested grand-mothers who loved to cook could perhaps be given a scholarship and a monthly stipend so that when their FFR training program was finished, they could continue to teach what they had learned to others in their community.

A Final Backstory

The successful move from a visionary idea to the actual launch of the First Food Responder program in January 2020 began with a fan letter that I wrote to a politician. It was the first and only fan letter that I have ever written.

I had been visiting family in California. One night, we were watching a local TV news show. A reporter was interviewing a local politician, Janice Hahn, the supervisor of Los Angeles County's District 5. She was talking about the importance of providing healthy meals to the elderly in her district.

When I was listening to the conversation between the reporter and Hahn, it seemed as though she was speaking directly to me. When the program ended, I quickly wrote down her name. The next morning, I called her office and asked if I could speak with her. The staff person who answered the phone invited me to send her an email instead. So I sent her an email to tell her that I welcomed her comments about importance of helping seniors eat better food. I included a link to our new website. If possible, could she write a testimonial?

I never received a response to my letter. Instead, she or someone in her office forwarded it to the head of a major agency in Los Angeles County. That single email, received by a county executive who also oversaw the county's Area Agency on Aging, became the match that lit the fuse for our rocket ride to success.

I received his call in March. Los Angeles County had just shut down 18 organizations that prepared food for vulnerable people in the county due to COVID-19. Could 23ZIP step in temporarily to help? He asked us to apply as a vendor and apply for a 10-week contract to provide emergency food service for the elderly. The county had also reached out with similar urgency to its network of existing vendors.

During the five-day wait, during which we registered as a vendor and received approval of our bid, Riverside County officials also reached out to us and talked of a potential multi-year meal service and delivery contract.

To date, we have signed three contracts with Riverside County for a total of $2 million. Over 22 months, we have prepared and delivered over 500,000 meals to vulnerable individuals including the elderly, individuals with health issues, and temporarily housed families in the county.

Our success has led to interest by the Behavioral Health Department of a major California university. They described a population of 80 clients who would benefit from our fresh, locally sourced, fiber-rich meals. We responded that our meals also include the potential for improved physical and mental health. Could these improvements and traditional social determinants of health be measured by them? This move beyond traditional patient care to nonmedical programs funded by Medicare, healthcare organizations, and philanthropy is cutting edge.

At age 78, I've had the lifelong opportunity to combine idea generation, innovation, business acumen, and team leadership in launching programs that combine passion and purpose with social good. The best practices gained over a lifetime, along with those of others, including the three visionary leaders have been combined to create the First Food Responders program.

So, dear reader, if you are interested in doing well by doing good, then what follows next is written with you in mind. It tells you everything you need to know about the First Food Responder program, including how to apply, how to volunteer, and how to contribute.

The next step is yours to take. You are being offered an opportunity to help the world take one giant step forward to achieving zero hunger. Ready to start?

Chapter 8

Get Involved as a Cook or Contributor

H ere is what makes us different.
Culinary arts schools, high school cooking classes, and private/internship cooking programs are designed for 16- to 24-year-old students and adults. These programs also include corporate- and food industry-funded programs. These job training programs run for several weeks up to several years and range from free to $20,000 or more.

Many job training programs include an introduction to culinary skills, online cooking and baking classes, food safety and hygiene courses for the catering industry, training in food industry roles and responsibilities, food handler certification, personal chef certification, food fermentation, science and cooking from haute cuisine to soft matter science, and kitchen chemistry.

While many programs include scholarships for job training, none includes the First Food Responder scholarship, stipend, mentorship, and training as a micro entrepreneur.

Your First Food Responder mentorship begins with an onboarding process. You fill out an online application (available at https://www.ziphomechef.com/become-a-ziphomechef). If you are already a licensed chef, you can begin after an initial review and understanding of our training protocol. If you are not yet licensed, you will be mentored through a 12-hour online course. The course requires that you successfully pass the final test. Additional training programs for becoming certified as a First Food Responder include emergency meal preparation, sanitation to COVID-19 safety levels, and food safety protocols.

To become a Level 2 Zipper, your training program will include micro entrepreneurship, marketing, and leadership skills. You are becoming a role model for others. We call this applied leadership. You are leading by example.

As a final step in our training program for Zippers, you will be asked to create a video of your home kitchen. You will be able to describe the steps you have taken for precertification as a home-based business.

Mentorship and ongoing support at the community level continues whether a home cook decides to serve as a paid or volunteer First Food Responder. Those who want to take the next step up and become a Level 2 Zipper will gain additional training in how to run a micro-business.

Whether you plan to open your own licensed microenterprise business at home (where it is legal to prepare meals in a certified home-kitchen), work in a commercial kitchen, or join the food industry workforce, you can always remain a First Food Responder. It's your choice. In the future, if 23ZIP receives a call for emergency meal preparation in your community, we will send out an invitation asking if you available for a short-term assignment.

The difference that distinguishes our innovative, personalized training program from all the others is that we focus on home cooks who want to be their own boss and at the same time enjoy a purpose-driven life in service to their community.

First Food Responders who join our brigade of home chefs already love to cook. They want to be valued for something they love to do. They also want to create their own menus, perhaps from secret family favorite recipes. Take, for example, 23ZIP's executive chef, Shad Finney. Part Cherokee, Finney comes from a three-generation restaurant family.

As a child, Finney grew up on the Walt Disney movie sets in Studio City, California. His grandmother was the personal chef for Walt Disney. She also served as executive chef to Disney studio executives and actors. Her dinner salads were Walt Disney's favorite. The meal plans that we serve to hungry families reflect some of the same ingredients that his grandmother served to Walt Disney.

This "first in the nation" approach to managing hunger and improving human health can be applied anywhere in the world where there is someone who loves to cook and hungry humans who need to be fed.

The 23ZIP Program

Level 1: First Food Responder Training Programs

Our First Food Responders are a zip code–based local network of distributed kitchens and individuals who are trained in food safety and who can respond on demand and act as volunteers with their cooking skills in an emergency.

This is our most basic introductory training for people with limited or no experience in emergency food service. Our two-month training program includes nutrition education, food safety training to federal standards, meal preparation, micro entrepreneurship, mentorship, licensing, and certification. Our entry-level invitation to home cooks is straightforward: "If you love to cook, have a home kitchen, and want to make enough money to pay your bills, join our army of home cooks. Become a First Food Responder."

Our successful commercial kitchen and home-based training program offers home cooks a stipend, scholarship, mentorship, and leadership opportunities.

Level 2: A Web-Based Technology Platform

Zippers are experienced chefs or individuals who have graduated from the First Food Responders training program, learned micro-entrepreneurship, and become certified. They want to work from home, continue to develop their skills, and run an independent food-service business on our technology platform.

Through our Level 1 training, they now have the skill sets to become a successful, independent microenterprise food business—a Zipper—on our tech platform, or choose to work in a commercial kitchen, restaurant, or other food-related business.

Level 3: Supported by Federal Food Contracts

Zippers who have graduated from a home cook to a federal-level cook and become star cooks can be invited to work as a FFR trainer, a professional chef, or a kitchen safety manager in one of our commercial kitchens that serves federal clients. This gives people a new level of faith in their cooking skills and ties all three levels together: from volunteer to certified home cook to professional chef.

How to Apply to Become a First Food Responder

The following offers a quick overview of our training program. It starts with a one-click choice of:

LINK A: Your online invitation to become a First Food Responder.

LINK B: How to volunteer your time

LINK C: How to contribute.

The Online Application: Home Cook/Referral/Volunteer/Contribute

In addition to your name and location, you will be asked how strong your interest in cooking is. Is preparing daily meals a necessity or a passion? What is your favorite cuisine? What kind of meals are a favorite for family or friends? Do you know others in your community who enjoy home cooking?

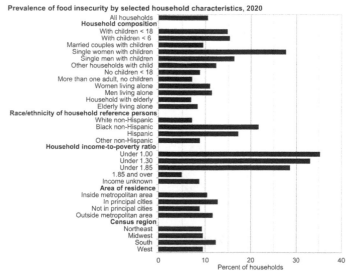

Prevalence of food insecurity by selected household characteristics, 2020

Source: USDA, Economic Research Service, using data from the December 2020 Current Population Survey Food Security Supplement, U.S. Census Bureau.

Cottage Food Industry Law vs. Utah's HB 94 MeHKO Law
In 2019, the Microenterprise Home Kitchen Operations law passed by a wide margin in the California state legislature. It was called "urgent to adopt." The law was then streamlined and updated in 2021 by the State of Utah, the second state in the US to adopt it.[78] In our opinion, Utah's MeHKO law represents the gold standard that all interested states should reference when creating their own MeHKO law.

ⓩ ZIPHOMECHEF™ | ⓟ 23ZIP

If You Love To Cook, We Need You!

23ZIP, a social enterprise is home to First Food Responders™ who are trained to prepare fresh, healthy meals for the food insecure in their own community. This may include the elderly, individuals with health issues seeking to eat better food, and children. Ready to start? **Visit ZipHomeChef.com.**

Strengthen Your Immune System With **Our Immune-Boosting, Anti-Inflammatory** Menu Planner and Food Prep Course offered as an ONLINE training program.

23ZIP.com offers workforce development and economic vitality training programs for people who **LOVE to cook** and have a home kitchen. What does it take to qualify for licensing as a Microenterprise Home Kitchen Operation. We are a social-impact public benefit corporation with 30-years experience in providing green, sustainable and healthy community solutions. We have you covered. We can work with you virtually to ensure the best learning environment for you to succeed!

23ZIP First Food Responders™ food and safety training includes plant-based, nutrient-rich lifestyle medicine diet. Check w/your Health Dept. to confirm the latest info.

ⓩ ZIPHOMECHEF™ | ⓟ 23ZIP

Seven Daily Steps for Home Cook Success

Daily habit formation is necessary to set and achieve high goals. Here are the seven daily steps that can be grooved into a daily habit by those who participate in our training programs. Mastering these seven habits can lead to success as a licensed microenterprise home-based business or to a future career in a local restaurant or related business in the food industry.

10 Food Safety Essentials

Everyone who takes their job seriously needs to follow safety rules related to the job they have. This is also true for becoming a licensed and certified home cook. We show you how to take food safety to the highest federal standards. We designed our food safety program to be the gold standard for kitchen safety.

Meal Planning Template

First Food Responders are independent contractors. They are paid for meal preparation through our federal, state, and local contracts and through philanthropy. Delivery is typically within one to three miles of their home or commercial kitchen. Where possible, FFRs are able to respond to emergency needs. In times of calm, they learn how to safely prepare their favorite meals to sell to customers on an online platform.

Nutrition Analysis Template

The 23ZIP proprietary nutrition analysis template enables Zippers to do an analysis of all ingredients that go into a meal they will prepare and sell. They create their own menus. They set their own price for the meals they prepare. Our online platform will keep track of the number of meals they sell per week. The limit is 60 meals. The licensed cooks affirm that all ingredients for every meal have been reviewed with food safety and potential allergens in mind.

Food Safety Daily Sign-Off
Like the Seven Daily Steps for Home Cook Success, you will use the daily food safety protocol for your home, or if you are using a ghost or cloud kitchen, you are required to use an app daily to confirm that you have completed the seven essential steps.

Five Vital Nutrients for Vegans
Did you know that a vegan diet needs to be carefully managed to avoid these five major health risks?
[see: Did You Know]

Onboarding Tutorial
This tutorial is designed for Zippers as they move from Level 1 training as First Food Responders to Level 2 licensed and certified cooks who want to create their own microenterprise MeHKO business on our online platform.

FFR Community Outreach
This is an optional leadership training course for those who want become part of a local food hub and engage in collabo-

How Microenterprise Law Works

Cottage Food Law		Microenterprise Kitchen
*(Packaged, Shelf-Stable) Current Law (AB1616)		*(Fresh Food/Meals) Utah 2021 (HB0094)
"Low-risk" foods that don't need to be refrigerated and usually don't make people sick like nut mixes, granola, cookies, candy, dry pasta and more.	**What**	Prepared meals and foods like cooked pasta, soup and tacos. Food cannot be cured or smoked, as a way of cooking. No oysters!
Pick up at your home or deliver to consumers. Or with a "class B" license sell to local retailers.	**Where**	Take out or eat in, at your home. no selling to other businesses. only delivery by you or family, not a service.
OK to have a promotional website. Foods need specific labeling. Local: No online ordering/ shipping.	**How to Sell**	OK to use an app or website to sell BUT there needs to be information for the consumer about the business and how to report problems.
$50,000 in annual gross sales (before subtracting expenses).	**$ Potential**	$50,000 in annual gross sales (before subtracting expenses).

23ZIP First Food Responders™ food and safety training includes plant-based, nutrient-rich lifestyle medicine diet. Check w/your Health Dept. to confirm the latest info.

rative projects with other organizations. They may even want mentorship to help them join a local board focused on food security as a volunteer.

Marketing Calendar
This propriety 23ZIP tool helps Zippers follow daily food trends and prepare menu options for community events such as tasting fairs and special holidays including Valentine's Day, Mother's Day, Father's Day, Fourth of July, fall harvest festivals, and the November to January holiday season.

Marketing Tutorial
As a licensed and certified Zipper, you will learn how to market your specialty foods to future customers, who may include friends, neighbors, organizations, and the home-based corporate workforce.

How to Market a Food Blog Post
This proprietary 23ZIP tool includes support for writing blog posts that follow trending food topics. It is designed to follow trends, specialty foods, ethnic and regional cuisine, and seasonal food choices.

Meal Planner
Did you know that your gut is a muscle? So is your heart. Do you know what foods exercise both? The *23Ingredients Meal Planner for Health, Wealth, and Happiness* has been tested and proven successful over 50 years. This single recipe—

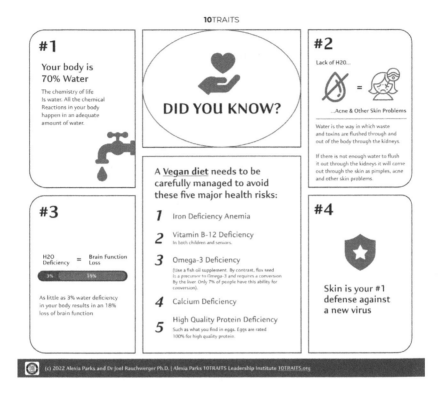

10TRAITS

#1

Your body is 70% Water

The chemistry of life Is water. All the chemical Reactions in your body happen in an adequate amount of water.

DID YOU KNOW?

A **Vegan diet** needs to be carefully managed to avoid these five major health risks:

#2

Lack of H20...

= ...Acne & Other Skin Problems

Water is the way in which waste and toxins are flushed through and out of the body through the kidneys.

If there is not enough water to flush it out through the kidneys it will come out through the skin as pimples, acne and other skin problems.

#3

$\frac{H2O}{Deficiency}$ = $\frac{Brain Function}{Loss}$

3%   18%

As little as 3% water deficiency in your body results in an 18% loss of brain function

1 Iron Deficiency Anemia

2 Vitamin B-12 Deficiency
In both children and seniors.

3 Omega-3 Deficiency
(Use a fish oil supplement. By contrast, flax seed Is a precursor to Omega-3 and requires a conversion By the liver. Only 7% of people have this ability for conversion).

4 Calcium Deficiency

5 High Quality Protein Deficiency
Such as what you find in eggs. Eggs are rated 100% for high quality protein.

#4

Skin is your #1 defense against a new virus

(c) 2022 Alexia Parks and Dr Joel Rauchwerger Ph.D. | Alexia Parks 10TRAITS Leadership Institute 10TRAITS.org

based on 23 Ingredients—is designed to boost your health and fitness, reduce stress, increase your energy, support weight management, reduce disease risk, and increase happiness.

The body thrives on consistency. The *23Ingredients* planner offers a twice-daily meal plan for all ages, across all countries and cultures. It creates a bridge between vegan, paleo, and ketogenic meals and combines the best of all three.

The planner offers food security at a time when climate change threatens grains such as wheat and corn crops with both drought and flooding. Most of these ingredients can be grown locally. It offers a path out of food poverty because the estimated $100 per person saved on this $5/day meal plan can be used to pay down credit cards, a mortgage, or a car payment, or deposited in a savings account each month.

Are you one of those people who is too unhappy to take time to be happy? Take heart. The *23Ingredients* planner was created with you in mind. Even if you don't have time to be happy, you do have time to eat. When you feed your microbiome its favorite food, it rewards you by producing 90 percent of your feel-good serotonin. You simply have to provide it with its favorite food and it will return the favor by lifting the corners of your mouth into a smile.

On this plant-based meal plan, you will even find yourself waking up smiling regardless of circumstances because you are changing your body chemistry one meal at a time.

Once you learn to shake off food, people, circumstances that don't match your goals, you will free yourself to be who you really are. Sounds easy? It's not. It takes focus, self-discipline, and courage to take this 21-Day Challenge. This book is offered free when you donate $100 or more. A contribution of $1,000 will provide a scholarship for training and the licensing fees for one First Food Responder.

Keep Yourself Healthy
Here are 10 steps you can take to protect your body against a deadly virus. It was developed by co-author Joel Rauchwerger, who has not been sick—not even with a common cold—in more than 50 years.

Protect Against Viruses in 10 Steps

10 steps to protect your body against a deadly virus

1 Make your skin your first line of defense

To keep your skin "well oiled" eat GOOD fats and oils like olive oil, avocado, butter, sour cream and high fat cheese and yogurt. For best protection against a deadly virus take direct action to avoid dry, cracked skin. To do this, you will need a healthy, well-oiled skin, both on the outside and also your interior system of skin (your nasal passage, mouth, & lungs, for example).

2 Keep your respiratory and digestive skin healthy

Your respiratory and digestive systems are invaginations of your outside skin. For example, your outer skin turns inward at your nose and mouth. So what goes for the outer skin also goes for inner skin.

3 Stay hydrated. Drink lots of water.

Remember to avoid drinking liquids such as water, tea, beer or soup during a meal. Drink water 20-minutes before or after a meal. A sip of water to help with swallowing food is OK. When the hydrochloric acid in your stomach is strong, it will dissolve protein and kill most viruses and bacteria on contact.

4 Keep your stress hormone cortisone low

The fastest way to reduce stress is through touch, such as massage including self-massage (neck, feet and hands). Or through meditation, yoga, or stretching exercises. The second fastest way is through aerobic exercise, non-stop exercise that boosts your heart rate for at least 10-60 minutes every other day.

5 Choose high quality protein to build strong antibodies

To support the rapid production of antibodies in your own body, eat high quality protein such as eggs or sardines first at each meal. Your stomach acid will quickly breakdown the protein into 20 amino acids and put them to work.

6 Take Vitamin B-12 sublingual 1x per week

Seniors need to take Vitamin B-12 under the tongue. Lack of sufficient Vitamin B-12 may result in pernicious anemia.

7 Eat soluble fiber daily to help detox your body

Soluble fiber is a prebiotic that your GUT Microbiome needs. A healthy Microbiome can detoxify your body up to 50%. Soluble fiber includes vegetables like spinach, kale, red bell pepper, onions, cabbage and zucchini. And fruit like apple, banana, orange, blueberries, grapefruit, raisins and more.

8 Help heal your gut with soluble fiber

Soluble fiber in your daily diet will help your GUT Microbiome produce short chain fatty acids (SCFAs), which heals the gut lining to prevent germs from coming in and putting your immune system on overdrive.

9 Meet in a large, ventilated room if socializing

If socializing, stay in a large ventilated room. Avoid sitting with others in small, cramped spaces.

10 Save money with soap instead of hand wipes

Soap does not kill germs; it washes them away. Wash your hands frequently; keep them away from your face.

(c) 2022 Alexia Parks and Dr Joel Rauchwerger Ph.D. | Alexia Parks 10TRAITS Leadership Institute 10TRAITS.org

About the Authors

Alexia Parks

A lexia Parks is president and CEO of 23ZIP, Inc., a public benefit corporation that is the home of the First Food Responders. She is an award-winning social impact entrepreneur who has launched 37 successful projects, including Votelink.com, one of the first electronic democracy websites on the Internet. For this breakthrough innovation, *Newsweek* magazine called her "One of 50 people who matter most on the NET."

Parks met Joel Rauchwerger in 2010 and has collaborated with him on a whole-body health and self-care series of videos and books.

A keynote speaker and author of 16 books, Parks formerly wrote for the national desk of the *Washington Post*. She was the first accredited blogger for the United Nations Framework Convention on Climate Change. She has also served as a United Nations mentor and founded the nonprofit Alexia Parks 10TRAITS Leadership Institute.

As a United Nations mentor, Parks was assigned to work with a young woman leader from the Global South. She served as a virtual mentor to Rehmah Kasule for 18 months. During the time of her mentorship, this young leader became *Fortune* magazine's number-one award-winning Social Impact Entrepreneur at their 2014 Most Powerful Women in the World Summit. The following year, Rehmah Kasule received a first-place award for creating "the most sustainable" program across the entire African continent.

At the 10TRAITS Leadership Institute, Parks developed a series of university-accredited training programs for corporate and organizational leadership and healthcare professionals. The Colorado State University Division of Continuing Education has accredited her online training programs.

Parks is recognized as a visionary thought leader and world expert on leadership and empowerment based on the synergy between 10 unique traits found in the brain. With a focus on trait-balanced leadership for improved decision-making, her breakthrough innovation and online tool is based on a dozen fields of science, including neurobiology, neuroscience, the neuroplastic brain, split-brain research, hormonal research, the psychology of perception, and both cultural and physical anthropology.

Joel "Rauch" Rauchwerger, PhD

Joel Rauchwerger, former faculty at Baylor College of Medicine in Houston, Texas, is a popular lecturer on preventative medicine, a scholar across many fields of science, and an athlete. He has had a lifelong interest in how to use fiber-rich, nutrient-dense foods and simple lifestyle changes to strengthen the immune system and help prevent, reduce, or reverse many physical and mental health problems. Rauchwerger is known for practicing what he preaches. He has not been sick—not even with a common cold—in more than 50 years.

In 1972, Rauchwerger received a fellowship from the National Institute of Health to fund his research at Baylor College of Medicine in the field in bone marrow transplantation. In 1974, he made a major medical breakthrough. His research showed a genetic resistance by bone marrow transplant patients to having another transplant, such as a heart transplant. His report was well received by a panel of world experts in the field, and his future in that specialized field of medicine looked bright.

However, his breakthrough research, which is still referenced today in the medical literature, drove him to focus on a bigger vision of human health and to pursue a career in preventative medicine. Instead of focusing on how to achieve a successful heart transplant, he decided to expand his understanding of food and lifestyle change that could prevent heart attacks or certain deadly diseases in the first place.

Rauchwerger continued his research at Baylor College of Medicine, and as a faculty member, used his vast medical knowledge to train future doctors and nurses. His teaching style was so popular with medical students that there was a two-year waiting list to get into his classes.

In addition to serving on the faculty, Rauchwerger also worked with well-known, world-famous cardiologist and heart surgeon Michael DeBakey. He was invited to join the team of medical doctors who worked on the case of the "baby in the bubble," in which a baby named David was born without an immune system. David's life story was later made into a movie starring John Travolta.

Today, what makes Rauchwerger unique in the field of whole-body health is his vast knowledge of science, medicine, brain function, nutrition, biochemistry, and psychology, as well as the fundamentals of good digestion, the microbiome, a ketogenic lifestyle, human psychology, stress management, and biofeedback.

A lifelong athlete, he has also developed an innovative all-ages workout program called the 640 Workout. It's a

10-minute whole-body fitness program that exercises all 640 muscles in the body, including the gut and the heart.

In collaboration with Alexia Parks, Rauchwerger has produced a 10-part medical library, 75 short educational videos, and numerous books that focus on self-care. Each offers a whole-body approach to physical and mental health and well-being, and is told with the skills of a scholar, educator, and master storyteller.

Acknowledgments

I am grateful to Christian, Hillary, Daniel, and Bianca for your love and support. I also appreciate the help of readers, including Marc Brenner, Woody Gair, Richard DelMonte, and Juliana DelMonte, who also consulted on program development, as well as Michael Ebeling, who offered welcome advice. I appreciate Dr. Joel Rauchwerger's partnership with me in creating this book.

Our thanks go to Larry Kirshbaum, who served as a reader and advisor and came up with the perfect subtitle. Thanks as well to our editors Lori Paximadis and Nancy Osa, and to Madissen Miller for her graphic designs included at the back of the book, and to Patty Williams, our First Food Responder Ambassador. Finally, we must recognize Riverside County

Housing and Workforce Solutions, Continuum of Care, and Community Action Partnership for providing the wind beneath our wings that launched this successful program.

Endnotes

1   Clare O'Connor, "Are Grocery Stores Doomed? Study Shows More Shoppers Buying Food at Target, Walmart, Pharmacies," Forbes.com, February 18, 2014, https://www.forbes.com/sites/clareoconnor/2014/02/18/are-grocery-stores-doomed-study-shows-more-shoppers-buying-food-at-target-walmart-pharmacies.

2   "'Food Deserts' Become 'Food Swamps' as Drugstores Outsell Major Grocers," UCLA Fielding School of Public Health, press release, June 8, 2019, https://ph.ucla.edu/news/news-item/2019/jun/food-deserts-become-food-swamps-drugstores-outsell-major-grocers.

3   "Food Deserts," Food Empowerment Project, https://foodispower.org/access-health/food-deserts; "Riverside

Food Sustainability Map," Grow Riverside, http://grow-riv.com/riverside-food-sustainability-map; Ashley Dean, "Here's Where Denver's Food Deserts Are, and What the City Is Doing about Them," Denverite, October 19, 2016, https://denverite.com/2016/10/19/denver-food-deserts.

4 Christy Brissette, "This Is Your Body on Fast Food," *Washington Post*, March 1, 2018, https://www.washingtonpost.com/lifestyle/wellness/sneaking-a-little-junk-food-doesnt-mean-all-is-lost/2018/02/26/828b75fa-1b36-11e8-9de1-147dd2df3829_story.html.

5 "Obesity and Overweight," National Center for Health Statistics, Centers for Disease Control and Prevention, https://www.cdc.gov/nchs/fastats/obesity-overweight.htm; "Mental Health and Substance Use State Fact Sheets," Kaiser Family Foundation, December 13, 2021, https://www.kff.org/statedata/mental-health-and-substance-use-state-fact-sheets.

6 Dasha Kolyaskina, "Kentucky Leads US in Per Capita Prescriptions Filled," Pegasus Institute, July 18, 2018, https://www.pegasuskentucky.org/post/2018/07/18/kentucky-leads-us-in-per-capita-prescriptions-filled-in-2017.

7 "Stress in America 2020: A National Mental Health Crisis," American Psychological Association, October 2020, https://www.apa.org/news/press/releases/stress/2020/report-october.

8 Jennifer Moss, "Burnout Is about Your Workplace, Not Your People," *Harvard Business Review*, December 11, 2019, https://hbr.org/2019/12/burnout-is-about-your-

workplace-not-your-people; Michael Beer, Magnus Finnström, and Derek Schrader, "Why Leadership Training Fails—and What to Do about It," *Harvard Business Review*, October 2016, https://hbr.org/2016/10/why-leadership-training-fails-and-what-to-do-about-it.

9   Michael Beer, Magnus Finnstrom, and Derek Schrader, "The Great Training Robbery," Harvard Business School Working Paper 16-121, April 2016, https://www.hbs.edu/faculty/Pages/item.aspx?num=50953.

10 "The Psychobiotic Revolution," Research Spotlight, University of Cork, Ireland, https://www.ucc.ie/en/research/spotlight/thepsychobioticrevolution.

11 23Ingredients is a universal, plant-based menu planner, where self-care is healthcare from the inside out; available at https://www.amazon.com/dp/1692197568.

12 "Prevalence of Food Insecurity by Selected Household Characteristics, 2020," Economic Research Service, US Department of Agriculture, https://www.ers.usda.gov/webdocs/charts/80061/insecurity.png?v=2582.2.

13 "Malnutrition," World Health Organization, June 9, 2021, https://www.who.int/news-room/fact-sheets/detail/malnutrition.

14 "Facts and Figures on Food and Biodiversity," International Development Research Centre, December 23, 2010, https://www.idrc.ca/en/research-in-action/facts-figures-food-and-biodiversity.

15 David Grotto and Elisa Zied, "The Standard American Diet and Its Relationship to the Health Status of Amer-

icans, *Nutrition in Clinical Practice* 25, no. 6 (2010): 603–612, https://pubmed.ncbi.nlm.nih.gov/21139124.

16 See Regeneration International's website: https://regenerationinternational.org/why-regenerative-agriculture.

17 Britt Hobo Days website: https://www.britthobodays.com/hobo-museum.

18 Eudie Park, "10 Iconic Wild West Figures," Biography.com, April 30, 2020, https://www.biography.com/news/wild-west-figures.

19 Alfredo Morabia, "Joseph Goldberger's Research on the Prevention of Pellagra," *Journal of the Royal Society of Medicine* 101, no. 11 (2008): 566–568, https://www.ncbi.nlm.nih.gov/pmc/articles/PMC2586852.

20 "Whole Grains: Hearty Options for a Healthy Diet," Mayo Clinic, August 20, 2020, https://www.mayoclinic.org/healthy-lifestyle/nutrition-and-healthy-eating/in-depth/whole-grains/art-20047826.

21 L. Kaul and J. Nidiry, "High-Fiber Diet in the Treatment of Obesity and Hypercholesterolemia," *Journal of the National Medical Association* 85, no. 3 (1993): 231–232, https://www.ncbi.nlm.nih.gov/pmc/articles/PMC2571875.

22 Alexia Parks, "Happy Hour Makes Bartenders and Bar Owners Happy. Here's What It Does to Your Liver and Your Gut," Medium, November 18, 2020, https://alexiaparks.medium.com/happy-hour-makes-bartenders-and-bar-owners-happy-heres-what-it-does-to-your-liver-and-your-gut-7f6603da82b3.

23 Benedict Carey, "Dr. Rita Levi-Montalcini, Nobel Winner, Dies at 103," *New York Times*, December 20, 2012, https://www.nytimes.com/2012/12/31/science/dr-rita-levi-montalcini-a-revolutionary-in-the-study-of-the-brain-dies-at-103.html.

24 "First-Ever United Nations Resolution on Homelessness," Department of Economic and Social Affairs, United Nations, March 9, 2020, https://www.un.org/development/desa/dspd/2020/03/resolution-homelessness.

25 "Homeless Population by State 2022," World Population Review, https://worldpopulationreview.com/state-rankings/homeless-population-by-state.

26 "The State of Mental Health in America," Mental Health America, https://www.mhanational.org/issues/state-mental-health-america.

27 Casey Newton, "Mark in the Metaverse: Facebook's CEO on Why the Social Network Is Becoming 'a Metaverse Company,'" Verge, July 22, 2021, https://www.theverge.com/22588022/mark-zuckerberg-facebook-ceo-metaverse-interview.

28 "Return on Environment: The Economic Value of Protected Open Space in Southeastern Pennsylvania," Summary Report, Delaware Valley Regional Planning Commission, https://www.dvrpc.org/openspace/value/pdf/ReturnOnEnvironment-TheEconomicValueOfProtectedOpenSpaceInSoutheasternPA-SummaryReport.pdf.

29 Jena Hilliard, "Social Media Addiction," Addiction Center, https://www.addictioncenter.com/drugs/social-media-addiction.

30 George Land, *Grow or Die: The Unifying Principle of Transformation* (Wiley, 1986).

31 Alexia Parks, *Parkinomics: 8 Great Ways to Thrive In the New Economy*, 2nd ed. (Education Exchange Network, 2010).

32 Soken-Huberty, "10 Root Causes of Homelessness."

33 "U.S. Billion-Dollar Weather and Climate Disasters," NOAA National Centers for Environmental Information, 2022, https://www.ncei.noaa.gov/access/monitoring/billions.

34 Emmaline Soken-Huberty, "10 Root Causes of Homelessness," Human Rights Careers, https://www.humanrightscareers.com/issues/root-causes-of-homelessness.

35 Parks, *Parkinomics*.

36 Jared Diamond, "The Worst Mistake in the History of the Human Race," Discover.com, May 1, 1999, https://www.discovermagazine.com/planet-earth/the-worst-mistake-in-the-history-of-the-human-race.

37 "Cuneiform," Khan Academy, https://www.khanacademy.org/humanities/ancient-art-civilizations/ancient-near-east1/the-ancient-near-east-an-introduction/a/cuneiform.

38 Jihed Abidellaoui, "Tunisian Enthusiast Recreates Sea Snail Purple Dye That Defined Ancient Royals," Reuters, February 8, 2022, https://www.reuters.com/lifestyle/odd-

ly-enough/tunisian-enthusiast-recreates-sea-snail-purple-dye-that-defined-ancient-royals-2022-02-08.

39 Richard W. Steiger, "Roads of the Roman Empire," https://pita.ess.washington.edu/tswanson/wp-content/uploads/sites/9/2018/10/Roads-of-the-Roman-Empire.pdf.

40 G. Michael Stathis, "The Crusades: A Modern Perspective on the 900th Anniversary of the Event," Medievalists.net, November 30, 1995, https://www.medievalists.net/2013/05/the-crusades-a-modern-perspective-on-the-900th-anniversary-of-the-event.

41 "Genghis Khan," History.com, November 9, 2009, updated June 6, 2019, https://www.history.com/topics/china/genghis-khan.

42 "Great Wall," in *A Visual Sourcebook of Chinese Civilization* (online), edited by Patricia Buckley Ebrey et al., University of Washington, https://depts.washington.edu/chinaciv/geo/twall.htm; "10 Facts about the Great Wall of China," History Extra, August 5, 2020, https://www.historyextra.com/period/ancient-history/great-wall-china-facts-history-length-why-built-from-space.

43 Andrea Briney, "A Brief History of the Age of Exploration," ThoughtCo., January 23, 2020, https://www.thoughtco.com/age-of-exploration-1435006; "5 Amazing Facts about the Mongolian Emperor Kublai Khan," *History Is Now*, December 2, 2018, http://www.historyisnowmagazine.com/blog/2018/12/2/5-amazing-facts-about-the-mongolian-emperor-kublai-khan; James Voorhies, "Europe and the Age of Exploration," Met-

ropolitan Museum of Art, October 2002, https://www.
metmuseum.org/toah/hd/expl/hd_expl.htm.

44 Holly Yan and Susannah Cullinane, "Canadian Government Invokes Emergencies Act due to Blockade and Protests over COVID-19 Measures," CNN.com, February 15, 2022, https://www.cnn.com/2022/02/14/americas/canada-truckers-protest-monday/index.html; Matt Egan, "US Business Leaders Sound the Alarm on US-Canada Border Blockade," CNN.com, February 11, 2022, https://www.cnn.com/2022/02/11/business/canada-trucker-protest-businesses/index.html.

45 Andy Kessler, "Putin's 'Vertical' Empire Will Fall," Wall Street Journal, March 6, 2022, https://www.wsj.com/articles/putins-vertical-empire-fall-ukraine-russia-business-kleptocrat-oligarchs-value-companies-11646581296.

46 Ivetta Gerasimchuk and Yuliia Oharenko, "Beyond Fossil Fuels: Fiscal Transition in BRICS," International Institute for Sustainable Development, November 2019, https://www.iisd.org/system/files/publications/beyond-fossil-fuels-russia.pdf.

47 Anna Kireeva and Charles Digges, "Permafrost Melt Caused by Climate Change Could Cost Russian Billions, Environmental Minister Says," Bellona.org, June 3, 2021, https://bellona.org/news/arctic/2021-06-permafrost-melt-caused-by-climate-change-could-cost-russia-billions-environmental-minister-says.

48 Thomas L. Friedman, "The Cancellation of Mother Russia Is Underway," *New York Times*, March 6, 2022, https://www.nytimes.com/2022/03/06/opinion/putin-ukraine-china.html.

49 Peter Yeung, "How '15-Minute Cities' Will Change the Way We Socialize," BBC.com, January 4, 2021, https://www.bbc.com/worklife/article/20201214-how-15-minute-cities-will-change-the-way-we-socialise.

50 Cheyenne Kabil, "The Bloom of Vertical Gardens," Medium.com, June 28, 2015, https://medium.com/cleantech-rising/the-bloom-of-vertical-gardens-a4c286e9b865.

51 Joel Rauchwerger and Alexia Parks, *23 Ingredients Menu Planner for Health, Wealth, and Happiness* (independently published, 2019).

52 Jemima Weber, "*Milked* the Documentary Is Here, and the Dairy Industry Might Not Like It," Plant Based News, March 25, 2022, https://plantbasednews.org/culture/film/milked-documentary.

53 "Mayor Adams, NYC Health + Hospitals Expand Access to Lifestyle Medicine Services City-Wide," NYC.gov, February 7, 2022, https://www1.nyc.gov/office-of-the-mayor/news/063-22/mayor-adams-nyc-health-hospitals-expand-access-lifestyle-medicine-services-city-wide.

54 Joel Garreau, *The Nine Nations of North America* (Avon, 1982).

55 Jillian Abbott, "New Yorkers Should Start Victory Gardens Today," *Daily News*, April 25, 2022, https://www.

nydailynews.com/opinion/ny-oped-start-your-victory-garden-today-20220425-aeir6uhqrjffnoielmfmvzgo64-story.html.

56 "The 10 Best Online Nutrition Certifications of 2022," Intelligent.com, March 28, 2022, https://www.intelligent.com/best-online-courses/nutrition-certification.

57 "Farmers' Markets Accepting SNAP Benefits," Food and Nutrition Service, US Department of Agriculture, May 5, 2022, https://www.fns.usda.gov/snap/farmers-markets-accepting-snap-benefits.

58 "Sustainability 2020," Sustainability.org, https://sustainability2020.org.

59 L. Kaul and J. Nidiry, "High-Fiber Diet in the Treatment of Obesity and Hypercholesterolemia," Journal of the National Medical Association 85, no. 3 (1993), https://www.ncbi.nlm.nih.gov/pmc/articles/PMC2571875; "Dietary Fiber Reduces Risk for Type 2 Diabetes," CardioSmart, June 3, 2015, https://www.cardiosmart.org/news/2015/6/dietary-fiber-reduces-risk-for-type-2-diabetes.

60 Masrul Masrul and Ricvan Dana Nindrea, "Dietary Fibre Protective against Colorectal Cancer Patients in Asia: A Meta-Analysis," *Open Access Macedonian Journal of Medical Sciences* 7, no. 10 (2019): 1723–1727, https://www.ncbi.nlm.nih.gov/pmc/articles/PMC6560290; Joel Rauchwerger, "The Human Biome and Why It Matters," YouTube, June 13, 2015, https://www.youtube.com/watch?v=7iRd_KmWJNI&t=1176s.

61 Adam Hadhazy, "Think Twice: How the Gut's 'Second Brain' Influences Mood and Well-Being," *Scientific American*, February 12, 2010, https://www.scientificamerican.com/article/gut-second-brain.

62 "Six Types of Exercises That Increase Neurogenesis," Sunwarrior, September 9, 2019, https://sunwarrior.com/blogs/health-hub/exercise-that-increase-neurogenesis; Brock Armstrong, "How Exercise Affects Your Brain," *Scientific American*, December 26, 2018, https://www.scientificamerican.com/article/how-exercise-affects-your-brain; Joel Rauchwerger, "Do This Daily to Improve Memory and Critical Thinking," YouTube, January 28, 2021, https://www.youtube.com/watch?v=T-BevpXt8hnk.

63 Angela Pereira, "Home Economics for a New Generation," University Affairs, June 9, 2008, https://www.universityaffairs.ca/features/feature-article/home-economics-for-a-new-generation.

64 "Mayor Adams, NYC Health + Hospitals Expand Access to Lifestyle Medicine Services City-Wide."

65 Juliana A. Donohue, Tracy Severson, and Lauren Park Martin, "The Food Pharmacy: Theory, Implementation, and Opportunities," American Journal of Preventative Cardiology 5 (March 2021), https://www.ncbi.nlm.nih.gov/pmc/articles/PMC8315372.

66 Dhruv Khullar, "Food for Thought—and Health. The Right Diet for Patients can Improve Outcomes and Reduce Costs," Washington Post, February 16, 2020,

https://www.washingtonpost.com/health/food-for-thought--and-health-the-right-diet-for-patients-can-improve-outcomes-and-reduce-costs/2020/02/14/015b22aa-4825-11ea-bc78-8a18f7afcee7_story.html.

67 L. Freese, "Human Ecology," *International Encyclopedia of the Social and Behavioral Sciences* (2001): 6974–6978.

68 "Timeline of UK Government Coronavirus Lockdowns and Restrictions," Institute for Government, https://www.instituteforgovernment.org.uk/charts/uk-government-coronavirus-lockdowns; "Shanghai COVID Lockdown: Fences Appear around Residential Buildings to Keep People in Their Homes as Strict Rules Continue," Sky News, April 25, 2022, https://news.sky.com/story/shanghai-covid-lockdown-fences-appear-around-residential-buildings-to-keep-people-in-buildings-as-strict-rules-continue-12597908.

69 Lisa Curtis, "Why the Big Quit Is Happening and Why Every Boss Should Embrace It," Forbes, June 30, 2021, https://www.forbes.com/sites/lisacurtis/2021/06/30/why-the-big-quit-is-happening-and-why-every-boss-should-embrace-it/?sh=4ee61f9e601c; "Holly Corbett, "How Companies Can Reverse the Great Resignation by Supporting Working Mothers," Forbes, April 21, 2022, https://www.forbes.com/sites/hollycorbett/2022/04/21/how-companies-can-reverse-the-great-resignation-by-supporting-working-mothers.

70 Kim Parker and Juliana Menasce Horowitz, "Majority of Workers Who Quit a Job in 2021 Cite Low Pay, No Opportunities for Advancement, Feeling Disrespected," Pew Research Center, March 9, 2022, https://www. pewresearch.org/fact-tank/2022/03/09/majority-of-workers-who-quit-a-job-in-2021-cite-low-pay-no-opportunities-for-advancement-feeling-disrespected.

71 Caroline Stowell, "Why Doctors Like Me Are Leaving Medicine," WBUR, March 10, 2022, https://www.wbur. org/cognoscenti/2022/03/10/a-doctor-shortage-is-looming-caroline-stowell.

72 Greg Rosalsky, "The Great Resignation? More Like the Great Renegotiation," *Planet Money*, National Public Radio, January 25, 2022, https://www.npr.org/sections/money/2022/01/25/1075115539/the-great-resignation-more-like-the-great-renegotiation.

73 Joseph Gyourko, "What's Going to Happen to All Those Empty Office Buildings," *Knowledge at Wharton*, February 28, 2022, https://knowledge.wharton.upenn.edu/article/whats-going-to-happen-to-all-those-empty-office-buildings.

74 "Generational Differences Chart," Learning and Talent Development, University of South Florida, https://www. usf.edu/hr-training/documents/lunch-bytes/generationaldifferenceschart.pdf.

75 Stephanie Neal and Richard Wellins, "Generation X—Not Millennials—Is Changing the Nature of Work," CNBC.com, April 11, 2018, https://www.cnbc.

com/2018/04/11/generation-x--not-millennials--is-changing-the-nature-of-work.html.

76 "Big Demands and High Expectations: The Deloitte Millennial Survey," January 2014, https://www2.deloitte.com/content/dam/Deloitte/global/Documents/About-Deloitte/gx-dttl-2014-millennial-survey-report.pdf.

77 Bill McKibben, *Deep Economy: The Wealth of Communities and the Durabel Future* (Henry Holt, 2007), 211.

78 "Microenterprise Home Kitchen Amendments," https://le.utah.gov/~2021/bills/static/HB0094.html.

A free ebook edition is available with the purchase of this book.

To claim your free ebook edition:

1. Visit MorganJamesBOGO.com
2. Sign your name CLEARLY in the space
3. Complete the form and submit a photo of the entire copyright page
4. You or your friend can download the ebook to your preferred device

 Morgan James BOGO™

A **FREE** ebook edition is available for you or a friend with the purchase of this print book.

CLEARLY SIGN YOUR NAME ABOVE

Instructions to claim your free ebook edition:
1. Visit MorganJamesBOGO.com
2. Sign your name CLEARLY in the space above
3. Complete the form and submit a photo of this entire page
4. You or your friend can download the ebook to your preferred device

Print & Digital Together Forever.

Snap a photo

Free ebook

Read anywhere